NO HOME FOR YOU HERE

FIELD NOTES

SERIES EDITOR: Paul Mattick

A series of books providing in-depth analyses of today's global turmoil as it unfolds. Each book focuses on an important feature of our present-day economic, political and cultural condition, addressing local and international issues. Field Notes examines the many dimensions of today's social predicament and provides a radical, politically and critically engaged voice to global debates.

Published in association with the *Brooklyn Rail*

Titles in the series:

A Happy Future is a Thing of the Past: The Greek Crisis and Other Disasters
PAVLOS ROUFOS

Hinterland: America's New Landscape of Class and Conflict
PHIL A. NEEL

No Home for You Here: A Memoir of Class and Culture
ADAM THERON-LEE RENSCH

NO HOME FOR YOU HERE

A Memoir of Class and Culture

ADAM THERON-LEE RENSCH

REAKTION BOOKS

Published by Reaktion Books Ltd
Unit 32, Waterside
44–48 Wharf Road
London N1 7UX, UK
www.reaktionbooks.co.uk

First published 2020
Printed and bound in Great Britain
by T. J. International, Padstow, Cornwall

A catalogue record for this book is available from the British Library

ISBN 978 1 78914 200 6

The leaders of the nation had fixed their gaze so long upon the illusions of a false prosperity that they had forgotten what America looked like. Now they saw it—saw its newness, its raw crudeness, and its strength—and turned their shuddering eyes away. "Give us back our well-worn husk," they said, "where we were so snug and comfortable." And then they tried word-magic. "Conditions are fundamentally sound," they said—by which they meant to reassure themselves that nothing now was really changed, that things were as they always had been, and as they always would be, for ever and ever, amen. But they were wrong. They did not know that you can't go home again. America had come to the end of something, and to the beginning of something else.

Thomas Wolfe, *You Can't Go Home Again* (1934)

Contents

Prologue: You Can't Go Home Again

On an uneventful day in 2010, amid the lingering fallout from the 2008 financial crisis, I entered Penn Station and boarded a train headed for Toledo, Ohio. For the next fourteen hours, the train snaked its way across upstate New York and into Pennsylvania, through a landscape of small, impoverished towns that seemed to have been forgotten by time. I had never been to these places, but they all seemed familiar to me, even comforting. My recognition was dim but instinctual—like having a word on the tip of my tongue, except instead of a word it was an entire way of life. The quiet struggle. The taunting but always elusive promise of success. The loneliness masquerading as prideful self-sufficiency. I *knew* these places, even if I didn't know their names.

During the 1980s, my family lived in a mobile home on Ohio Township Road 215, a desolate stretch of pavement between the small city of Findlay and the much smaller village of Arcadia. We had moved our mobile home there from a trailer park, from which we had been evicted for not paying rent (my parents had withheld rent to protest conditions in the trailer park, a strategy that didn't have its intended result). At the time, we were part of the "working poor," predominantly lower-class families still struggling from the recession earlier in the decade. My mother worked a variety of part-time jobs: seamstress, waitress, door-to-door saleswoman for Mary Kay cosmetics. My father worked at a wholesale pizza outlet and a bottling factory. Neither had finished college: my mother, studying to become a social worker, was asked by her father during her sophomore year to come home and take care of her younger sister, who at the time ran with petty criminals and was consistently getting in trouble with the law; my father, an idealist with dreams of writing the next great American novel, dropped out after his freshman year to satisfy his romantic wanderlust. (This brief period of road travel in the late 1970s seems now a quaint anecdote from an unrecognizable past, when relatively low oil prices, combined with a dollar that had roughly four times the purchasing power it does today, made it much easier for someone with little money to wander the country aimlessly.) Politically, my parents were both left-leaning, though my father—influenced by the writings of Henry David Thoreau, Jean-Jacques Rousseau, and Karl Marx—was much more out- spoken about his views. He liked to argue with his factory coworkers about foreign policy and social injustice, and in his spare time, he wrote letters to the local newspapers criticizing the Reagan administration and championing the civil rights of the poor, the oppressed, and the otherwise forgotten.

Today, our family would almost certainly be lumped in with the so-called "white working class," that large but poorly defined group of individuals whose poverty, despair, and resentment have become fashionable topics for pundits and journalists. With our mobile home, our Midwestern country attitude, and our deep rural and working-class background, we checked almost every box of the stereotype. Despite this, we did not live the sad, despairing life imagined by and represented in today's media. We struggled financially, but we were, in a word, happy. My father biked to work and wrote short stories and his letters to the editor. My mother shopped at discount stores and bought fabrics to mend or make clothes. As she told me recently, "We never had any money. But we had a lot of fun." During the summer, my sister and I ran wild and swam in a small pond behind our trailer. Our father took us for rides on an old John Deere lawn mower. We had cookouts and parties with our large extended family. The whole world seemed to smell like beer and charcoal and freshly cut grass, though it also sometimes smelled of dead leaves, gasoline, and fertilizer from the nearby farms. Occasionally, the sulfur in our water made everything stink like rotten eggs, but we learned to accept this as a part of life. It was just the way things were, which is to say that neither my sister nor I had any reason to question our poverty, and the way of life it made possible for us.

As I peered out from the train two decades later, now in my mid-twenties, my recognition of rural life was much more complicated. I'd been living in New York City for the past few years as a young graduate student with plans to publish a novel that never materialized. I survived for a while on student loans that were quietly accruing interest, and eventually took work at a couple of bookstores and as the personal assistant for a critically acclaimed poet. It was a month-to-month existence, but, nevertheless, it allowed me to live out my fantasy: I was an "intellectual," an artist who saw the world for what it truly was, and who was savvy enough to find beauty in its ugliness. I may have been no richer than in Ohio, but I had access to a wealth of social and cultural capital that had never been available to me, and that acted as a marker of a privileged class status. I shopped at co-op food markets and spent afternoons contemplating works of art. I read Marx and Hegel in artisanal coffee shops and was surrounded by a rich, diverse community of writers, actors, and artists, many of whom shared my interests in politics and the avant-garde. Giving this world up meant more than moving from an apartment in Brooklyn to my mother's spare bedroom in Ohio. It meant losing the hip, cultured veneer that separated me from my trailer-park past.

The train arrived, after much delay, in downtown Toledo. The Amtrak attendant made his way from car to car announcing the station, and those of us departing gathered our belongings

and shuffled towards the exits. It was early but already warm as
we stepped down and dragged ourselves, sleepless and irritable,
into the bright, humid morning. I stood at the street and had a
cigarette while I waited for my mother to pick me up. Nearby, a
woman cursed into a payphone—her air conditioner had stopped
working, and she couldn't sleep through the night. Much of
Northwest Ohio was settled on the Great Black Swamp, and
the air sticks to you, some days, like wet paper.

Toledo's Amtrak station is located next to the muddy banks
of the Maumee river. The building was opened to the public in
1950 as a shining example of postwar investment, designed as
an homage to the city's powerful glass industry. But like other
industrial hubs in the Rust Belt, Toledo went into a decline during
the 1970s and '80s as manufacturing slowed and capital flowed
outwards into the bordering suburbs, where big-box retailers
and neighborhoods of cul-de-sacs and tree-themed streets filled
the metropolitan area. Wealthier, predominately white residents
moved out of the city, dramatically shifting its demographics.
In 1940, Toledo was 94 percent white; as of 2010, it was only 64
percent white, with a segregated neighborhood layout that has
pushed most minorities into and around downtown. Overall,
Toledo's population has decreased by 50,000 in the last two
decades, mirroring the losses of other Ohio cities like Cleveland
(120,000), Cincinnati (65,000), Dayton (40,000), and Akron
(25,000). While the city has experienced the start of a slow
renaissance, the effects of these changes are still palpable. You
can almost feel the desperation, a bleak and quiet sense of loss.

My mother finally arrived to pick me up. Heading south, away
from the city and into the farmland many associate with Ohio, the
drabness of concrete and steel gave way to the flat, open landscape. As we made our way back through the mixture of small
towns and villages and in-between places that make up most of
the area, I saw the depressing, unrefined image so many have
of rural America: miles of corporatized farmland, cheaply built

houses and decaying trailer parks, supermarkets and chain restaurants smashed into sprawling strip malls. I was in the middle
of nowhere, surrounded in every direction by flyover country that
is as easy to dismiss as it is to exploit for political points.

Despite its familiarity, rural Ohio now struck me as a strange,
hostile place. There was nothing here—no bookstores or bodegas,
no literary events packed with eager young writers attempting
to impress agents with the details of their satirical novels. There
was just the horizon, the telephone poles, and the neighborhoods
of mobile homes and prefabricated houses that had been put
together somewhere else. All the things that once seemed comforting about my simple, Midwestern upbringing now stirred in
me only disgust and cynicism. Looking out the window, I was
overwhelmed by contempt: it was all a trap, a massive, stupid
fraud orchestrated by a monstrous network of exchange that
cared only for maximizing profit.

I did not know this place. Although I could name the streets,
and find my way around the network of nameless country roads,
I could not go home again. Whatever was waiting for me there
would not be what I remembered.

What we call "home" might seem obvious: where you live, where
you grew up. Amid the flux of life, it is the constant that keeps
you moored. It is a city, a state, a country. Home, for me, has been
a number of places: my childhood homes, apartments in small
Ohio towns and in cities like Chicago and New York where I
have lived as a struggling writer and academic. Sometimes home
is just the Midwest, or the rural farmland that stretches from
Ohio to Illinois, its vast network of highways and county roads
I have driven aimlessly in the summer months, wondering when
the humid air might become too saturated and empty itself in a
sudden downpour. But "home" is also something bigger and more
meaningful than all of this. Home is an idea, a promise of stability
and comfort. It is where we feel we most belong, a place where

problems can be easily solved and everyday life makes sense. Embedded in the concept of home is a nostalgia for a simpler time, a better way of life we look back upon as a solution to the problems and dissatisfactions of the present. As with all nostalgia, this remembrance is at once hopeful and melancholic: we can never actually recapture that past. As the novelist Thomas Wolfe wrote,

> You can't go back home to your family, back home to your childhood, back home to romantic love, back home to a young man's dreams of glory and of fame . . . back home to aestheticism, to one's youthful idea of "the artist" and the all-sufficiency of "art" and "beauty" and "love," back home to the ivory tower, back home to places in the country, to the cottage in Bermuda, away from all the strife and conflict of the world, back home to the father you have lost and have been looking for, back home to someone who can help you, save you, ease the burden for you, back home to the old forms and systems of things which once seemed everlasting but which are changing all the time.[1]

Writing in the 1930s, Wolfe witnessed how the Great Depression forced the country's population to reevaluate its ideas of prosperity and success, supposedly guaranteed by the free market. More than an economic crisis, the Depression was an ideological crisis that left many Americans wondering what had become of the country they thought they knew, their home, with its "old forms and systems of things which once seemed so everlasting."

As the 2016 presidential election and its aftermath have shown, America is experiencing a similar crisis. We have not experienced a rupture in the status quo so much as seen its purest realization, and the strangeness of the past few years has revealed the fecklessness of procedural norms that have long structured our political imagination. We have, in Wolfe's words, "come to the end of something, and to the beginning of something else." What this "something else" is has yet to be determined, but what has become clear is that many people no longer feel at home, and many others have never found the home they thought they were promised. They have looked around and wondered where it is they belong, and what kind of life there is left for them in an age of draconian cutbacks and normalized austerity. They are desperate and outraged, and for good reason. A living wage is exceedingly rare: the national minimum wage has stagnated since the early 1970s, and as of 2016 the median wage was only $30,533, meaning half of all wage earners made less than this; roughly 30 percent brought home an annual income of less than $15,000.[2] Despite a brief slump following the 2008 subprime mortgage crisis, housing is more expensive than it has ever been, its costs far outpacing inflation. President Obama's 2010 landmark legislation, the Affordable Care Act, made some headway into slowing down the rising costs of health care, but it did very little to assuage the deep anxiety surrounding access to medical treatment, a fact compounded by the jump in health-care premiums that took place in 2017. College, once the path to a prosperous life, has become instead a risky investment, its prohibitive costs ensuring a near lifetime of debt that has prevented many from achieving financial stability—and kept even more from enrolling in the first place.

Added to this, the political process has become futile, exhausting, and alienating to most Americans. The large number of people who don't vote, especially within the working class, is indicative of a deep distrust in a two-party system that many see as failing them. The influence of outside money, albeit a well-worn scapegoat, cannot be overstated: elections are transparently corporatized, and the power of the average voter appears minuscule relative to that wielded by elite donors and lobbyists (consider the many failed attempts in recent years to pass gun-control legislation despite overwhelmingly popular support for it). Perhaps this is why Hillary Clinton's deep ties to this broader establishment, framed as expertise and experience by her supporters, represented for many complicity in a bloated, nepotistic bureaucracy. Despite her qualifications, she embodied the image of partisan politics that reeks of inefficiency, self-interest, and gridlock. Donald Trump's comically blasé attitude on the campaign trail, meanwhile, struck many as more sincere. He portrayed himself as a man who could not be bought (contra Clinton, who, fairly or not, was criticized for receiving large sums to give speeches to financial institutions whose power she claimed she would curtail), and his eagerness to break from political and social conventions promised a refreshing departure from the old way of doing things.

Since Trump's inauguration, not surprisingly, little has changed for those hoping he might shake up politics on Capitol Hill. His "champion of the forgotten man" image and "draining the swamp" rhetoric have proven to be the crass opportunism they always were, and his policies—from the Tax Cuts and Jobs Act to his partial repeal of the Dodd–Frank Act—have consistently favored wealthy business elites over working-class voters. Nevertheless, he has enjoyed fierce support from his Republican base, and the fact that he still retains such favorable ratings reaffirms, for many, a common assumption:[3] his base, and the broader resurgence of populist politics in America, is driven not by rational political and economic demands but by fear, anger, and disgust. Consider Trump's slogan, "Make America Great Again." One way to read this language is as a form of dog whistling, signaling a nostalgic return to the postwar economic boom of the 1950s that was as segregated as it was prosperous. So, while Trump has done very little economically for his working-class supporters, he has satisfied their nativism by making good on his anti-immigrant rhetoric, strengthening the power of u.s. Immigration and Customs Enforcement (ice) and imposing a travel ban on passengers from a number of Muslim-majority countries.

It is undeniable that America is experiencing a revival of proud and visible white supremacy, fomented online by a generation of alienated young men, and that the conservative movement to which Trump has become a kind of savior ingratiates itself with those who support cruel, authoritarian policy. But several things are worth examining when attempting to understand this trend's relationship to economic hardship and populist resentment of elites, as well as the trend's impact on Trump's surprise victory and continued popularity. Trump's most fervent support came not from poor whites, as has popularly been suggested—complete with visuals of haggard factory workers and mobs of overweight hillbillies in tacky outfits, all indulging in tasteless displays of jingoism and white identity politics. Trump's strongest support was from people like Richard Spencer, the handsome, well-educated white supremacist who inherited wealth from his family's cotton-farm business. To be precise, according to the American National Election Study, two-thirds of Trump voters reported a household income of greater than $50,000.[4] For a married couple, of course, a combined $50,000 is still working class, but it cuts against the image of the Trump voter as fundamentally "poorer" than Clinton's base of presumably middle-class or wealthy professionals. As Jesse Myerson wrote for *The Nation*, Trump's real base is middle-class and affluent whites who are "taken in by Horatio Alger stories" and "haven't won 'big league,' but they've won enough to be invested in the hierarchy they aspire to climb."[5]

This confusion surrounding the working class has long been the case. Barbara Ehrenreich, writing in the late 1980s, notes how in their "discovery" of the working class, middle-class professionals were quick to associate blue-collar workers with authoritarian personality traits and "backwards" beliefs, no doubt to secure their own class position as the gatekeepers of professional knowledge. But, as she points out:

> Thanks to the work of historian Richard F. Hamilton, we now know, for example, that Nazism was not a movement

of the "masses"—the lower middle class or working class—
but received its strongest backing from wealthy urbanites
and landed gentry. Similarly, Hamilton has shown that other
notorious outbreaks of "authoritarianism" and intolerance,
such as lynchings in the American South or McCarthyism in
the 1950s, tended to be initiated by the wealthy and only later
embraced by the lower classes.[6]

Despite what was portrayed as almost self-evident by journalists
across the spectrum, this trend hadn't changed by 2016. In a
study by the Public Religion Research Institute (PRRI), published
in conjunction with *The Atlantic*, the authors note, "Those who
reported being in fair or poor financial shape were 1.7 times more
likely to support Clinton, compared to those who were in better
financial shape."[7] The more telling economic factor was not
hardship, but what the authors describe as "fatalism," or the belief
that one's financial situation would not improve and would perhaps
get worse. Rather than actual economic hardship, *perceptions*
of one's socioeconomic status prove to be more powerful—
especially among those with some money—and undoubtedly lead
to "economic anxiety" (the key feature of anxiety being that it is
oriented towards the future, in anticipation of an expected event).
When reported by *The Atlantic*, a decidedly centrist outlet, these
economic findings were largely dismissed in favor of a familiar
narrative: "white working-class voters who say they often feel like
a stranger in their own land who believe the u.s. need protecting
against foreign influence were 3.5 times more likely to favor
Trump than those who did not share these concerns." Indeed,
the prominent abstract offered by *The Atlantic* was that "societal
change, *not economic pressure*, motivated votes for the president
among non-salaried workers without college degrees."[8]

It should be noted that from the outset this study focused on
Trump's support within the "white working class." After all, this
is who op-ed after op-ed told readers was the driving force

behind Trump's success. But who is the white working class? The PRRI defines this demographic as "white, non-Hispanic Americans without a four-year college degree who hold non-salaried jobs." Some voters fitting this description did, of course, vote for Trump, but as broader data reveals, fewer than half of Trump's votes came from this demographic—hardly overwhelming support. This means that the study excluded Trump's base: middle- and upper-class whites who have significantly more to lose than their wage-working counterparts, and who are more likely to be driven by a fear of waning social status that can easily find comfort in far-right, fear-stoking ideas. As Myerson notes, the middle class has anxiety "associated with paying taxes; with jealously guarding their modest savings; with stopping black people from moving nearby and diminishing the value of their property and thus the quality of their kids' schools; and with preserving the patriarchal family structure that facilitates it all." Poor wage-workers, meanwhile, generally have little or no property, minimal savings, have a different relationship to taxes, and are, in fact, no more likely to hold racist beliefs than those with money.[9] In short, they have very different economic concerns: they want a secure job with a living wage and benefits, not a tax write-off for their business expenses.

One reason the middle-class support for Trump is often neglected might be that "class" as a concept is so poorly defined. The PRRI study consistently writes of "white working-class" voters in opposition to "white college-educated" voters, a categorization that overlooks the plurality of working-class whites who have obtained college degrees but nevertheless remain mired in poverty—the growing pool of young adjunct professors, for example, who despite their coveted and often expensive graduate degrees have found themselves making less than $30,000 by cobbling together teaching gigs with no benefits and no job security. Excluding these individuals from the working class is an astonishing oversight, and perpetuates an arcane, postwar understanding of the working class: white men, typically, who work in the industrial sector as factory linemen, construction workers, miners, and other professions traditionally associated with physical or "hard" labor. Not surprisingly, we have come to think of class in terms of physical attributes and cultural affiliations associated with these professions, often divorced from any material and historical conditions—the working class is whoever "looks" and "acts" working-class.

A goal of this book is to offer a different picture of what it means to be working-class (full stop), one that has nothing to do with how we look or act, or how we might identify ourselves culturally. To do so, I rely on an understanding of class that is material, centered around how work comes to define and guide our lives in a myriad of ways—the "work" of the working class. The most important thing to note at the outset is that while labor provides workers with an income, class is not actually defined by this income.[10] There are, of course, rough correlations between one's income and one's class position, as well as between one's income and one's educational pedigree, but these can be misleading. Income is an abstract marker that ignores the kind of labor one performs, as well as the broader circumstances that make this income possible. It is entirely possible to have a low income and nevertheless possess a significant amount of wealth (if, say, it is inherited, as it often is), just as it is possible to hold no college degree and nevertheless be enormously successful. Conversely, one can imagine an hourly worker with a decent income (say, $25 per hour) possessing very little overall wealth and even struggling financially due to significant debts and high costs of living, especially if those debts belong to the larger $1.6 trillion student loan debt or $1 trillion credit card debt. Instead of using income or education to distinguish between classes, I use ownership of capital—the material resources used for the production of business, including investment and employment of labor. When conceived this way, class division is primarily between those who control and allocate economic resources (banks, corporations, stockholders, and the sympathetic representatives they fund) and those who must sell their labor power in exchange for a living (workers). The former belong to the capitalist class, while the latter constitutes the working class.[11]

The poorly understood middle class, which many conflate with the working class, occupies a contradictory place in this material account of class: their modest holdings and lack of passive income might be perceived as working class, while their activities as potential stockholders or employers (small business owners) might situate them more properly in the capitalist class. It is precisely their contradictory position, one which aligns them at times with the working class and at other times with the capitalist class, that makes them so attractive to politicians. Rarely do politicians explicitly court the poor or the wealthy; it is predominately "the middle class." It is *this* class that is "shrinking," according to progressives. It is the financial struggles of *this* class that Republicans feign sympathy for in a ridiculous attempt to appear in touch with "average Americans." Not surprisingly, the common usage of the term "middle class" in politics and everyday vernacular has nothing to do with this contradictory relationship to work and profit. It is usually a term denoting either the middle-third of income distribution or the cultural markers of "living comfortably" that this income makes possible: a modest and well-kept home, a newer car, a summer vacation, perhaps an occasional luxury purchase. In many ways, the middle class is a political fiction, one perfectly malleable to any politics so long as it is divorced from its relationship to the other two classes it straddles. This is not to say that the middle class "doesn't exist" so much as it is to say the way we talk about the middle class says nothing about class, and very little about work.

Thinking about class in terms of work rather than income or culture is advantageous because it highlights the major disparities in power that structure American society and reproduce

inequality. While there are gradations of privilege between
the working and middle class, from the service worker making
$21,000 to the retail district manager making $100,000, these
two workers have more in common with each other than either
of them does with the CEO of their company. The manager lives
a more comfortable life, to be sure, and likely has the privilege of
receiving benefits not available to the service worker; but both
work to maintain their existence (rather than, say, receive inflated
compensation or shares in stock, or own property that provides
passive income through rent), and neither has control over the
material resources used for the employment of other workers
(the manager has some power, but primarily acts on behalf of
his or her boss). It is in the latter difference, between those with
significant power and those without it, that class war becomes
most visible. In their attempt to maintain this relationship, those
in power prevent us from creating a better society. It is also this
difference that often pits many middle-class voters against the
working class: small-business owners struggling to compete with
larger corporations have a reason to support a radically conservative economic agenda, as many of these policies are written for
them. Given the need for their own labor to maintain operations,
they may also see themselves as self-made, and for this reason,
resent or look down upon so-called "handouts" that otherwise
aid the poor and the working class. Indeed, the middle class has
historically functioned as a kind of "cushion" separating the capitalist and working classes, to both protect capital and marginalize
attempts at cooperation among workers in the fight for power.

The other advantage this definition of class provides is that
it allows for a better understanding of the daily lives of working
people. As someone who, by all accounts, fits the profile of the
"white working class," I do not understand nor associate with this
rather meaningless label in any way, and I would guess that most
working-class whites feel similarly. Over the last few years, I have
seen the term countless times, first in articles written by supposed

experts, then by pundits narrating the tumultuous election, and then again by experts writing books and reflections on the unlikely turn of events that took place on November 9, 2016. I suppose, in this way, this book is not so different. But as I have read the many articles and books on the "white working class," I have noticed that they are rarely written by people who survive month-to-month on a wage, people who live in the regions they attempt to analyze and expose by uncritically accepting this label. While I don't mean to suggest they are all out of touch (though some are), they often fail to capture what it is like to live in those places, surrounded by those people who are not ethnographic subjects, but rather friends and family. They do not understand how it feels to call those places home. As a result, they tend to treat the "white working class" as a monolith, as a distinct group of human beings motivated by the same hopes and fears: "white, non-Hispanic Americans without a four-year college degree who hold non-salaried jobs." Even if we accept such a crude definition, this demographic is still extremely diverse. Working-class whites are waiters, teachers, realtors, and factory workers; they live in mobile homes, houses, and apartments; they are conservatives, libertarians, progressives, or simply indifferent to politics because they understand that few politicians have ever much looked out for anyone but themselves.

The other goal of this book, then, is to deconstruct the concept of the "white working class" and reveal it for what it is: a useless, misleading term, an appendage of our vulgar culture wars used by those who imagine poor and working-class whites are either an embodiment of a decaying past or a representative of our country's worst tendencies (or, nostalgically, "authentic" creatures who embody a conservative work ethic lost after decades of affluence and handouts have made us weak). I have long been surrounded by these struggling white workers, people who, like me, have been unable to fathom a life with money, and who have yearned to escape the class into which they were accidentally born, but which our society has insisted they naturally deserve. I myself have tried, and failed, to leave these people behind, but have found myself coming back to them, again and again, filled with a mixture of shame and sorrow. In what follows, I write about growing up in a rural part of the country, a white-trash kid whose cultural perceptions of privilege influenced what he imagined was his "way out." I tell this story not because it's special or particularly unique. I tell this story—my story, and the story of those around me—precisely because it is not unique, and because the history in which it unfolds is a history that weighs upon the present. My trajectory is common, one that many readers will recognize: a slow, agonizing climb with numerous missteps and financial setbacks; optimism, excitement, and yearning, punctuated by frustration, depression, and utter indifference.

For my entire adult life, I have, like my parents, lived pay-check to paycheck, carrying a mass of credit card and educational debt that has become a permanent fixture, but which has paradox-ically made my life "easier" in the sense that it has deferred my destitution for another day. Where I part from them is that I have achieved a level of education very few have, a marker of privilege that many in my community, including some in my family, have held against me as proof of my elitism and snobbery. According to them, I should be so lucky to have been able to attend school, to spend my days reading and writing and contemplating philosoph-ical problems instead of doing "real work." And in a certain sense, they aren't wrong: I have been lucky. But what took me a long time to realize is that these old distinctions—between types of labor that count and types of labor that don't—are based on cul-tural stereotypes that prevent us from recognizing that we belong to the same class. Our enduring and curiously seductive culture wars have encouraged people like me to look down on those they perceive as uneducated and backwards, just as it has encouraged those in rural and working-class communities to see people like me as out of touch and arrogant. Personal resentment of this kind is not in itself a "political" problem; it quickly becomes one when those in power exploit our antagonism to reframe the terms of the debate to exclude our shared class position, slowly but persistently making a dignified life more difficult to achieve by encouraging us to imagine we have little in common.

It is worth noting that all of this is especially true for, and keenly felt by, people in my generation. As a millennial, I belong to a generation that has developed a heightened awareness of inequality. Our familiarity with and reliance upon social media has generated a contentious, very public discourse around the recognition of cultural, sexual, gender, and racial identities. This discourse has splintered left politics into antagonistic camps: those committed to a politics of identity, for whom inequality can't be "reduced" to an economic register (even if they recognize its importance), and those who insist on the universality of class politics as a means of building solidarity across identities. I belong to the latter camp, and will argue that the only path forward is through a reassertion of class politics that does not make identity or culture central to its organizing logic. For those suspicious that such claims are either indifferent to marginalized identity groups or actively harmful to them, I can only ask that you read in good faith. As I will argue, class politics is not the specter of a twentieth-century labor movement of mostly white men (the working class today is predominately non-white); class politics is a coalition of workers who recognize that they have more in common than their divergent identities might lead them to believe, and that the wielding of their collective power against their common enemy—the capitalist class—is how they liberate themselves from oppression.

My generation has lived through a remarkable transformation of society, driven by an insidious doctrine those in power have championed with great indifference to the suffering it causes. While no generation is "freed" from these developments, those born after 1980 have no memory of a world not built by Reagan's radical economic agenda. We are an index, of sorts: historical witnesses to an unprecedented rise in education and housing costs that has made an already-precarious life more difficult, more frustrating, and often incredibly hopeless. The job market is dismal, and many have found themselves in a rapidly changing and brutally exploitative gig economy to make ends meet. We are less anxious about our future than we are fatalistic, and in our darker moments, we have accepted that we may die without ever shoveling ourselves out of debt. Some, including myself, have considered an early death as a reprieve from what usually seems like an empty, unfulfilling future.

But—and this is crucial—people my age belong to the future, which is to say that it waits for us. We *are* the future. This does not mean we will be able to create a better society, and it does not mean our generation is inherently more class conscious. Yes, some in my generation have begun successfully to run for office, and their victories have been cast as advancements for working people. But as we continue to protest, write, and organize, it remains to be seen whether we will overcome the failed strategies that have prevented a true working-class movement from establishing itself, or if we will merely allow history to repeat. As we do, it must be with an understanding that capitalism is an unjust, immoral, and inefficient system, and that the various tales we were taught by the Reagans, Bushes, and Clintons are merely justifications for those in power to maintain it. As we do, we must remember that we cannot go back home—to market growth, to Third-Way governance and "fiscal responsibility," home to bipartisanship and "opportunity" and the American Dream. This is not because, as for Wolfe, there is some idealized past beckoning us, one that we must leave behind. There was never anything there to begin with, only an imagined prosperity that very few enjoyed at the expense of workers like us: exploited and under-appreciated servers, cashiers, office grunts, gig economy serfs. We cannot go home again, but if we work together we can begin to build one. A better one, to be sure, than the mansions and gated estates we have never been allowed to enter.

one

The Era of Big Government Is Over

The first time I recognized I was poor I was in first grade. It was the early 1990s. Somewhere in a reunified Germany, chunks of the Berlin Wall had become souvenir kitsch, and one day an unremarkable piece fixed to a commemorative plate appeared in our home. I didn't know what it was, really, or why it was suddenly sitting in our living room. I used to touch it, wondering what was so valuable about a piece of cement that looked like something I might find in a parking lot or behind an old building. Perhaps my mother appreciated the novelty of it, the way it gave you something real, something material—not a picture of the wall, but a part of the wall itself. Maybe it was its nearness to history, as though by proximity our small home in Ohio could partake in the myth of prosperity sweeping across the world: capitalism and liberal democracy, those twin pillars of freedom, had reunited a torn nation. Who wouldn't want to be a part of that? To feel, even briefly, that things were going to work out for them, too?

Our family had always been far from greatness, at least of the material kind. My mother's father worked for Columbia Gas, and my father's father and brother worked for Cooper Tire & Rubber. According to nineteenth-century census records, earlier generations—my great-grandparents and their siblings—were simply "laborers." Some worked in the oil industry, and many others were farmers that lived in the greater northwest Ohio region after immigrating to the United States from Germany. We were not tycoons of industry, or even the kind of people who ambitiously climbed the ranks. We clocked in, we clocked out. We started families. We switched jobs. We borrowed money and went into debt. We saved for our children, hoping that things might somehow be less difficult, less exhausting. But when I was born, this was never certain. Even factory work, which had always been the closest thing to a guaranteed income in our part of the country, was getting harder to find.

My father worked second shift at Sundor, a juice plant owned by Procter & Gamble, and in the morning he would attend classes at Findlay University—he was going back to finish the degree he'd abandoned as a teenager in search of a romantic life. He often drove me to school, and some days it was the only time I'd see him. He had a 1974 Chevy Camaro that many would now admire, but at the time, I felt strangely embarrassed to be seen inside it. The interior had a peculiar smell—one I can only describe as artificial, or stale—and the upholstery was torn in places, dotted with cigarette burns. The exterior was light blue, not a hip black or white or red, and had dark blue, pencil-thin decals I would peel back when he wasn't looking. My father was rough on the transmission, which meant that it lurched forwards and occasionally stalled at stoplights. He listened to loud music, mostly hypermasculine rock, and enjoyed playing an exaggerated air piano on the dashboard. When he finally dropped me off at Bigelow Hill Elementary, I always hurried inside, concerned the others in my grade might witness what kind of father I had, and what kind of car he owned. Somewhere, deep inside of me, a light slowly flickered on: other people had nice things, and my family did not.

I was too young really to understand the complexities of class, or even fully grasp what being poor meant. I just understood there was a barrier of some sort, a gossamer wall that separated me from kids whose parents were doctors or managers or vice presidents of the factories where members of my family worked, kids who lived in large houses and rode in shiny new cars. Now, it seems to me foolish to care about these things, but as a six- or seven-year-old, I intuitively grasped that they seemed to matter to everyone else, and therefore should matter to me. Although I didn't have a language to express this, I felt it acutely as shame. Tugging at the secondhand clothes my mother had laid out for me in the morning, I would move through my day with a heightened awareness of myself. I began retreating into myself, adjusting my posture in hopes I could somehow become smaller and less visible.

Despite all of this, I was never completely unpopular. My parents were both gregarious—a useful skill they had cultivated in the service industry and dealing with bosses—and had shown me how to interact in public settings, how to compensate with charm what I lacked in social standing. I managed to make friends easily as I grew older, including many from wealthier families, but I tended to gravitate to those who were "different" in some way: the vulnerable and the shunned, which in our community usually meant the poor and non-white. Highly sensitive, neurotic, and anxious, I closely identified with outcasts, the loners and the targets of bullies. But I also wanted somehow to belong to that crowd of the beautiful and naturally gifted. I wanted to impress them, and I longed for the ease with which they seemed to move through the world, an ease that, even as a child, I understood was connected with status. Torn between these two worlds, I never really felt as though I belonged.

Although I didn't realize it yet, I never would.

I was born in the spring of 1984, a few months before Ronald Reagan cheerfully declared it was "morning again in America." That same year, HTLV-III (later renamed HIV) was identified as the virus that caused AIDS. The deadliest mass shooting (so far) in u.s. history took place in San Diego, California, when 41-year-old

James Huberty, armed with a shotgun, an Uzi, and a pistol, killed 21 people and injured nineteen others at a McDonald's restaurant. Crack cocaine hit the streets of Los Angeles, and in New York City, a white man named Bernhard Goetz shot four black teenagers attempting to mug him on the subway, igniting a national panic about urban crime that further inflamed racial stereotypes. After a long slump, unemployment finally returned to the pre-recession rate of 7.2 percent in November, and that same month Reagan defeated Walter Mondale at the polls, winning every state except Minnesota in a decisive victory for conservatives. Four years earlier, Reagan's criticism of government as "the problem, not the solution" had resonated with a country emerging from the murky waters of the 1970s,[1] which had witnessed a stagnating global economy that produced two major energy crises. Now, he had been given another four years to continue his supply-side agenda. Reagan's first legislative victory, the Economic Recovery Tax Bill of 1981, had slashed taxes on the wealthy from 70 to 50 percent, and within the next few years taxes for the wealthiest would fall to just 28 percent.[2] Reagan would make other cuts as well—to taxes on capital gains, to public services and government programs (knocking people off food stamps, eliminating Carter's jobs program, changing the criteria for Social Security), and to regulations overseeing a variety of institutions (one factor contributing to the Savings and Loans Crisis that broke out in 1986). After decades of New Deal regulation, conservativism seemed to have won. It was a glorious time to be a cultural conservative, and an even better time if you were rich.

My parents were young and recently married when I arrived just before Easter: my mother was 26, and my father was only 23. They had met just a year and a half earlier when my mother was waitressing at the Fort Findlay Playhouse and my father was trying to become an actor, delivering pizzas on the side to make money. My mother was a single parent at the time, raising a two-year-old daughter—my sister Tasha, who took a liking to our father and accepted him as her own (she was born in 1980, two months before Reagan won his first election, against Jimmy Carter). My parents originally planned to wait to get married, but when they discovered they were expecting a second child, they pushed up the date, my father found his job at Sundor, and they moved into the basement of my grandfather's house to save money. Like many poor couples, my parents relied on their family to get by: my mother's father, Wendell Theron Russell, would watch my sister and me many nights, and my father's father, Jerry Lee Rensch, was to loan them the money they needed to move from the trailer park and into the country over the next couple years.[3]

Although my earliest memories of the trailer park and the countryside date from the late 1980s, I came of age in the 1990s, that curious decade between the collapse of Communism and the fall of the World Trade Center. It was, at least on paper, a peaceful, prosperous time for the United States, a time when, for a poor family like ours, "making it" seemed as possible as ever. Despite a recession early in the decade, all the markers of a thriving economy were present: a continuous rise in GDP, job growth, low inflation, and a thriving stock market, driven partly by growth in the technology sector. The Internet was becoming a household utility that promised a utopian world of immense freedom, personal expression, and abundant profits. In 1995, Bill Gates launched a revamped version of Microsoft's signature Windows operating system, complete with advertisements featuring The Rolling Stones' "Start Me Up," a raucous, playful song that served as an anthem for the era. Even Bill Clinton's sex scandal, as fraught as it was with accusations of white-trash morality, seemed sardonically appropriate: a personal, indulgent use of power that mirrored the engorged profits of multinational corporations and their self-satisfied CEOs.

In some ways, things seemed to be looking up for us as well. My father was optimistic his education would allow him to escape the drudgery of factory work, and he and my mother moved us out of our mobile home in the country and into something that looked like a real house. After saving up, they'd purchased—for $50,000, on a rent-to-own basis—a small yellow ranch at the very north end of Findlay, Ohio. Compared to the mobile home, this house seemed huge: 1,140 square feet (106 sq. m), three bedrooms, and a basement we would eventually finish and turn into a family room. We built a bar there, with a refrigerator that was always stocked with cases of Sunny Delight my father brought home from the factory (he received them for free if the bottles had errors). In the far corner of the basement, my father set up a small writing desk with the electric typewriter he used to write his many letters and short stories. In one letter written around this time, titled "An Elite Class Makes America's Decisions," my father railed against "the authoritarian state" and asked pointedly, "Isn't it wrong that less than 1 percent of the population owns over 80 percent of the corporate wealth, and that a handful of millionaire politicians in Washington—our 'representatives'—have made it possible?"[4] Like many working people, my father understood that the political milieu of the United States was first and foremost one of careerism, and that politicians, by and large, were less interested in helping the poor than they were in paying lip service to win elections.

The neighborhood where we had moved was working-class, and most of our neighbors were families with kids. Every house on the block looked identical—the cookie-cutter approach developers commonly utilized when slapping homes together during the postwar housing boom. Although a quiet neighborhood, it was not an area where anyone with money would choose to live, and the pervading stench of white trash seemed to follow us. There was a small park nearby, but adjoining the neighborhood to the north, as you left the city limits, sat an unsightly Dow Jones Chemical factory that made plastics,[5] and through many of the properties ran a busy railroad line used for transporting raw materials and consumer goods. Living this close to it guaranteed a near-constant thrum of noise and a nagging fear that one of the kids running around might accidentally fall in front of an oncoming train.

I loved these trains, and they became a huge part of my childhood. At night, I would lie in bed and listen to the rattle of freight cars as they clamored through the darkness. The tracks were so close that I could walk from the back door, cross our backyard, and touch my hand to the warm metal in a matter of seconds. During the day, my sister and I would often walk the tracks, balancing on the rails as if we were walking a tightrope. Eventually, the rails would begin to vibrate and we would have to jump to the side and let the trains pass: massive diesel engines dragging steel beams, stacked automobiles, graffiti-covered boxcars, and oil tanks and coal. Sometimes we would place pennies on the tracks to flatten them, and if we were lucky, a friendly conductor might acknowledge our frantic demands, as we ran briefly beside him, to sound the whistle.

Criss-crossing the country, these trains carried many of the goods and raw materials that made up our economy and eventually found their way into supermarkets and car dealerships and newly constructed buildings. I bore witness to it, each day, this frenetic energy of circulation and reproduction. I felt the literal engine of capitalism in my chest as it passed by with its monstrous, indifferent force. Train after train, day after day, our country made itself again, the same as it ever was and always would be.

One September afternoon in 1992, my sister and I were told that President Bush would be riding past our house on those tracks. After the recession and a blundered attempt to topple Saddam Hussein's regime during the Gulf War, the incumbent president was campaigning partially on a vintage train he named *The Spirit of America*, no doubt to drum up a bit of patriotism. He made whistle stops almost exclusively in Ohio and spoke from the back of the old caboose. The image was calculated, cloaked in a veil of romance and nostalgia for the rural frontier, for the seemingly timeless myth of prosperity and development. Like Reagan before him and Clinton after him, Bush used this train not because he wanted to reinvest in America's train infrastructure—it had been years since the federal government had seriously invested in passenger rail, opting instead to give massive subsidies to the aviation and automobile industries—but simply because it looked nice. The image of an old train invoked pleasant buzzwords like "innovation" and "exploration," breathing life into the dying promise of prosperity. Trains remained a wonderful symbol of America's iconic expansion west, a beautifully crafted feat of engineering, inspiration, and determination that resonated with the broader optimism about free markets that came after the fall of the Soviet Union.[6]

My sister and I certainly didn't understand any of this at the time. We also weren't aware of our father's vehement contempt for Bush's policies, which he had been not-so-quietly expressing in the local papers. We were just excited someone so well known would grace us with his presence, that he would bother to come to this part of the country, to pass through our little town of mostly unremarkable people. Our neighbors all down the block ventured outside as well—some of them were almost certainly Bush supporters—and we all stood close to the tracks and peered into the distance. As the train approached at a slow pace, we could see President Bush standing at the back, leaning out and waving to supporters and disinterested observers alike. When he passed our yard, he looked at my sister and me and smiled. "Hey, kids!" he shouted.

He waved, and before we could think of something clever to shout in return he disappeared behind our garage and was gone. Photographs in the archives show his stop 20 miles (32 km) down the tracks in Bowling Green, where I would one day go to college, his arm outstretched at the small crowd of rural Ohioans. Perceived by many as an Ivy-league elitist, and more seriously viewed as indifferent towards the suffering of poor Americans after vetoing a generous Unemployment Insurance Reform Bill in 1991 and making it acceptable for employers to discriminate racially against potential employees, he was there to show everyone a kinder, gentler man.[7]

Although my parents were not moved by his presence, my sister and I were briefly transfixed. In school, I told everyone in class that I had talked to the president. It was an exaggeration of the truth, but one that felt as natural as it did necessary. I hoped this nearness to power would change the way others saw me. I hoped I could carry a part of Bush's fame around like a chunk of the Berlin Wall, and would thus somehow be redeemed: I wasn't just a poor, trashy kid, I was also "interesting." I was someone you might want to know. It was a nascent experience with navigating the confusing world of social status, attempting to parlay something useless into something valuable, a type of cultural capital that was not exchangeable for money or goods but could be used to set myself apart from every other poor kid in second-hand clothes. I had moved a tiny rung up the social ladder, or so I wanted to believe.

The reality is that none of this really mattered outside of my own perception of myself, which was distorted by a yearning to feel as though I belonged. My family had made small inroads into financial stability, but we were still struggling. After finishing his bachelor's degree, my father quit his job at Sundor because he assumed his education would guarantee him a better salary that, as it turned out, was not so easy to find. He was unemployed for almost a year, and after sending out resumes and not receiving word back, he returned to the factory, only to find out that it would be closing in a wave of corporate downsizing.[8] Eventually, he would find a job as a copywriter for an electronics company and, later, as a headhunter for a human resources firm, where his job consisted of pairing out-of-work laborers with companies that had available positions—glorified service work, essentially, that forced him to sit in an office all day on the phone. His modest income did not, to say the least, make it easy to pay back his student loans on top of his other bills. My mother, meanwhile, had been attempting to make a name for herself as a realtor, and managed to keep us afloat while my father was out of work. After a life of service industry work, she had been drawn to real estate in the mid-1980s by its promise of lucrative paychecks and the ability to "make your own schedule." She and my father couldn't afford consistent child care, and this allowed them to stagger their schedules so that one of them would be able to stay home to watch my sister and me when our extended family members weren't available.

For my mother, becoming a realtor had the added advantage of being much more respected than her older gigs as a waitress or house cleaner. But although real estate presents itself as a middle-class profession, it is at its core no different than service industry work. Realtors only get paid if they sell houses, and while an initial 3 percent commission on a $200,000 house seems comfortable—roughly $6,000 for one house, or $12,000 if you "double dip," meaning you both list and sell the house and thus receive two separate commissions—the structure of real estate depletes this quickly: realtors pay broker's fees and office fees, and are generally required to front expenses out of their own pockets (not to mention the number of days and weeks it takes to sell a house). Realtors are not guaranteed health insurance or retirement benefits, and are often dependent upon the accidents of the housing market to catch a big sale. While most real estate agents are affiliated with an agency that can help with exposure and referrals, the nature of the work is fundamentally individual. Most realtors slowly build their own client base and hope for word-of-mouth referrals to supplement paid advertising. The appeal of "making your own schedule" is that hours are flexible, but the reality is much less ideal: as with most service-oriented jobs, realtors are left to the capricious demands of their clients, and if these aren't satisfied quickly there's a chance the client may find a more responsive realtor. This means that realtors are in competition with each other, further compounding feelings of financial uncertainty. My mother's income was often punctuated by hot streaks followed by months with only a modest sale, a small-scale iteration of the larger boom-and-bust cycle that markets reproduce. Few professions are as intimately bound up with the broader economic trends of a society as real estate: its core asset, property, is fundamental to capitalism and the production of profit, and is directly affected by the Federal Reserve's decision to lower or raise interest rates (as the 2008 subprime mortgage crisis and its "recovery" showed).

Additionally, as a woman in real estate, my mother was often subjected to the scrutiny of her physical appearance, and was regularly placed in vulnerable situations by meeting with clients alone in empty houses (without a union, there was little for her by way of institutional protection). Before my mother purchased a business phone line, the number listed with her advertising in newspapers and on billboards was our shared house line. Strange men often called our house at all hours after seeing her photograph, and more than once I found myself listening to a man's voice whisper lewd remarks in my ear. While such attention disgusted her, she needed to maintain appearances because, as crass as it seemed, she knew it helped her attract more business. The nicer she looked, and the wealthier she appeared, the more her clients were inclined to believe she was successful and thus could be trusted. But as much as she longed to find a different profession, my mother put up with all of this. She drove hundreds of miles a week to show houses, often with very little notice, and always with the threat of not getting paid. She did it because she had no other choice: she didn't have the luxury of going back to school, especially now that my father had lost his job, and with two kids and a growing collection of debts, she couldn't risk switching careers. This was what she did now. It was who she was. And so she kept chasing after the next break, the next big listing that would let her breathe a little bit easier, for a little while, until she needed to do it all over again.

My parents' experience was hardly unique. Our family belonged to a broader demographic of working-class whites, what many called the "new white working class" that emerged in the 1980s and early 1990s. Unlike the postwar generation, these workers were not easily finding jobs in traditional blue-collar industries like manufacturing. Instead, working-class whites were more likely to be employed in the service industry and in white-collar office settings, often as a sales or customer service representative, and usually for lower wages than in the manufacturing sector. Despite the relative stability of the decade as a whole, rising productivity and continued GDP growth only marginally lifted wages of hourly workers, and these raises were certainly not enough to counteract the effects of inflation. In 1971, the minimum wage was $2, which, at that time, was sufficient to lift a family out of poverty. By 1991, the minimum wage had more than doubled to $4.25, but that same family would now fall well below the poverty line. If wage raises had kept up with inflation alone, the national minimum wage would have been over $6. Factoring in rising productivity, which, in theory, should have also raised wages, the minimum wage in 1991 should have actually been closer to $8. In total, nearly one-fifth of workers were being paid wages too low to lift a family out of poverty.[9]

In most respects, the economic trends of the 1990s remained in line with the broader restructuring of the labor force that had been taking place over the last few decades, defined by several key shifts that marked the end of the New Deal era: trade union membership, never high to begin with, declined dramatically;[10] traditional manufacturing work that once offered a living wage employed fewer and fewer workers, despite continued increase

in output; as a result, the service economy became a much
larger proportion of overall available jobs, which, as mentioned,
offered mostly precarious work that lacked benefits; new technologies increased productivity but wages stagnated and effectively
decreased due to long-term inflation; corporate tax rates
remained low while defense and military spending increased,
ballooning the deficit and necessitating cuts to social services and
various entitlements. In short, while the overall economy "grew"
in terms of crude numbers, workers did not see any significant gains. Many even experienced losses: one other crucial factor
in the growth of the economy during this time was the increase
in household debt, which allowed for the continued consumption
of goods and provided an opportunity for banks to turn interest
payments into massive profits.

In one of my father's most passionate letters, he wrote about
some of these issues remarkably deftly, expressing the anger and
frustration many in the working class felt at the time—towards
a self-interested Congress, towards big business, and especially
towards "crony capitalism" (or, capitalism). As someone who
lived this, who lost his job and struggled to find employment
that would help support his family, my father felt the effects
of inequality on a deeply personal level. His words are a time
capsule, untouched by the broader "prosperity" story told by
many historians, and give an immediate look into the concerns
of working people:

> As recently reported by *The Courier*, Rep. Mike Oxley once
> again graced Findlay with his presence at a Rotary meeting,
> and once again he claimed that the economy is booming "in
> the second year of Bush recovery." More important to the
> people of Findlay, however, is not what Oxley did say, but
> rather what he didn't say.
>
> What Oxley didn't say is that, first and foremost, he
> is a demagogue. His rare appearances in Findlay are for

self-centered political gain, nothing more. His goal as a public official is not tending to the concerns of all the people of his district, but rather the pursuit of power, prestige, and endless perks that come with the job—at the expense of our hard-earned money.

What Oxley didn't say is that fully 90 percent of the 365,000 jobs created in the month of February were either part-time or temporary jobs that paid minimum wages and no benefits. In fact, since 1982, full-employment has grown less than 20 percent while temporary employment has increased nearly 250 percent. By the year 2000, labor leaders project that half of the entire American workforce will be temporary workers, exploited at low pay and denied health benefits.

What Oxley didn't say is that these 365,00 new jobs created will merely increase the ranks of America's "working poor"—people employed 40 hours a week (or more) at such low wages that they are unable to be self-sufficient. At any given time they lack one or more of the basic necessities: food, clothing, shelter, medical care. According to the Current Population Survey, as of 1990 some 56 million people—23 percent of America's population—had fallen into the abyss of the working poor.

What Oxley didn't say is that the American ethos (responsibility and hard work lead to success) is failing miserably. People are working, but more and more of them are unable to get ahead, are often unable to afford basic necessities just to live. There is no "Bush recovery." In fact, despite the opinion of many economists, all evidence indicates that the American economy is getting worse, not better. Corporate giants like GM, IBM, Sears and Boeing are in the midst of massive lay-offs—hundreds of thousands of jobs have been eliminated since 1985, and more losses are coming.

What Oxley didn't say and will never admit is that he and fellow congressmen—both Republicans and

Democrats—represent the wealthy interests that are the demise of American capitalism. According to the *Washington Post*, more than 70 percent of each party's campaign contributions come from corporations. The implications of the fact are staggering. The rampant greed and short-term profit motive of corporate elites have moved industry out of the country, forced remaining labor wages to decline with the cost of living, and public officials like Oxley have allowed it to happen merely so they can be re-elected!

One need only look to Toledo, Lima, or Fostoria to see the results of a deteriorating free-market economy. Findlay continues to prosper, but it is by no means immune from similar disaster. We must distinguish between the deceiving talk of politicians and simple truth.[11]

It is uncanny to read my father's letters now, many of which could have been written today, with minimal to no changes. This is not a testament to how much smarter my father was than everyone else, or to his ability somehow to presciently imagine the future. It is a sobering indictment of an economic system that hasn't changed. It is also a recognition that those who live and struggle to survive in poverty understand the nature of this system more quickly than those who don't, and on a more intuitive level. They understand how it works, which is to say whom it benefits, because they are routinely subjected to its whims, to its capricious cycles of stability and crisis. They understand that so-called economic growth has no relationship with their everyday lives, and that it is entirely possible for an economy to grow with none of the benefits "trickling down" to them. Indeed, this is the fundamental logic of capitalism, despite relative increases in quality of life over time: while the stock market breaks records, this is hardly a benefit for working-class people who have no wealth to invest in stocks, and it certainly doesn't reflect in any meaningful way the rate and quality of employment. During the presidencies of Reagan, Bush, and Clinton, the stock market soared, all as social services were reduced to pay for tax cuts and increased military spending.

When Bill Clinton was elected in 1992, he did so with the support of many working-class whites like my mother and father, especially from the Midwest, where he won every state except Indiana.[12] He also won big with union households, despite his tepid embrace of labor (he described himself as a "pro-worker, not anti-union" candidate who needed to "address both union and non-union" workers).[13] He was young and charming and spoke the language of a "new" Democratic party, a pro-business language that more progressive liberals like Jesse Jackson and Ted Kennedy rightfully recognized as capitulation to the demands of corporate America. Both his "invest and grow, not tax and spend" talking point and his claim that "the era of big government is over" would prove to be defining characteristics of his presidency. But Clinton's campaign, now widely known for the slogan "It's the economy, stupid!", played well with workers who did not benefit from the economic agenda of Ronald Reagan, and his humble beginnings allowed him to distinguished himself from the privileged life of George H. W. Bush. While certainly hesitant (a considerable chunk of working-class whites were drawn to Perot's strong economic nationalist platform, while others neglected to vote at all), the working class seemed ready to try something new. And so, on November 3, 1992, Bill Clinton and Al Gore, two young politicians from southern states, became the new voice of the Democratic party.

It might seem obvious, but I have few memories of these world-historical events: the radical changes enacted by Reagan and Bush, the end of Communism and the start of the Gulf War, the ongoing AIDS crisis, the recreation of countries that once belonged to the Eastern bloc. Even if I was conscious of these things, or heard about them in the news, it was always already filtered through a powerful local lens. I was a poor kid living in Ohio, after all, in the twilight of an America before everyone had Internet access. My contact with the world around me was limited to the local newspaper, whatever television programs we received, and a landline I used occasionally to talk with friends on the other side of town. Despite new technologies slowly beginning to connect the world in ways that were previously unimaginable, my own world was incredibly small. I could not fathom what lay beyond the flat horizon of the Ohio cornfields, which seemed to extend to the far reaches of the earth. Instead, I retreated into my imagination. My father encouraged me to read science-fiction and popular horror novels—Stephen King, especially, whose writing I fell into for hours at a time—as well as classics such as Jules Verne and Mark Twain. He also introduced me to the music of Nirvana and INXS, and taught me how to draw. Slowly, my father was nurturing my intellect and creativity.

When I wasn't reading or drawing or wandering the railroad tracks, most of my time was spent with aunts and uncles and cousins. My mother's side of the family was large, and because three of her sisters all had children roughly the same age, our families spent a lot of time together (between the four sisters, there were nine children, all born within ten years of each other). We got together many weekends at my Grandpa Russell's house on Frazer Street, which he had built sometime after the war for very little money. It was a simple, two-story house with a garage and an apple tree in the backyard. It had a peculiar, musky smell, and the upstairs rooms, which broke off from a long, central hallway, were dark and narrow. Some of us thought the house was haunted, perhaps by our Grandma Russell, who was a binge-drinker and died in 1972 in the downstairs bedroom. That was when my mother, at the age of fourteen, took on the role of matriarch for her two younger sisters, and assumed the duties of cooking and cleaning while their father worked on gas lines for the city.

For most of his life, Grandpa Russell was a heavy drinker and smoker. At one point, shortly after his wife's death, he was cited for driving under the influence, and according to my mother, he was very violent in the years before he got sober. Once, at the dinner table, he threw a fork so hard it stuck in my grandmother's arm (the abuse was mutual: she once cracked his head open with a high-heeled shoe). He eventually quit drinking and smoking, and by the time he began to babysit my sister and me while our parents worked, he was suffering from diabetes and glaucoma. His table always had artificial sweeteners on it instead of sugar, and as a late-night snack, I'd tear open a few pink packets and dump them into my cereal. He was slowly losing his eyesight, having suffered from both severe myopia and a detached retina, and often called his children by the wrong name. He had rough cheeks and a mustache, and whenever he kissed me goodbye, my own cheeks would hurt for a few minutes. If I stayed the night, which I sometimes did, I'd sit with him in the darkened living room while he watched *60 Minutes* or some other news show until I fell asleep listening to reports on Yugoslavia and Kosovo and a man named Milošević—few voices defined these years quite like those of Tom Brokaw and Dan Rather.

We had most of our holiday celebrations these years at Grandpa Russell's house. The kitchen was filled with hearty food such as chicken pot pie, sloppy joe, and baked corn dishes, and in my memory, football always played on the old boxed television in the living room. My father and uncles watched any game that was on, but like many in the region, their team was the Cleveland Browns—a losing team, historically, one that had shined for a brief decade in the 1950s and had barely approached success ever since (they would soon be moved to Baltimore by the team's owner, and for several years in the late 1990s, the Browns would not exist as a team). In a way, their trajectory seemed appropriate: we could root for the underdog, the team that got jerked around, as a way of championing ourselves. After all, what else did we have to celebrate but near-wins? We had no accomplishments, no great success story, at least not in the larger scheme of things. Cleveland's traditionally blue-collar fan base, with its rowdy celebration in the end zone bleachers, seemed to reflect back to us ourselves: hard-drinking and loud-mouthed, they were determined to have a good time regardless of their losses.

That was who we were, or at least who we told ourselves we were: a poor family with its share of tragedies and pain, but which somehow always managed to come together and have fun. Steadily, as the nights progressed and the adults loosened up with drinks, everyone barked laughter and smoked cigarettes on the porch and cursed their bosses and their jobs through another plate of food. My grandfather liked to take out his false teeth to frighten the grandkids, and inevitably someone would open up a package of fresh pantyhose and pass them around for a ritual called "hoseheads." The joke involved wearing the pantyhose over our heads like masks, the way a robber might to conceal his identity. The taut fabric would press our faces into grimacing, cartoonish expressions of horror. It was a simple thing, but somehow the absurdity of it all—the way our disfigurement had been transformed into something less terrifying in its clownishness—seemed to everyone the funniest thing imaginable. At the end of the night, we would all depart and return to our respective homes, briefly uplifted.

On Christmas Eve morning in 1992, Grandpa Russell had a stroke while driving his car. He lost control of his small sedan and crashed into the side of a house. He died a short time later in the hospital, less than three weeks after his 78th birthday. In the weeks that followed, our otherwise tight-knit family was strained by fighting over his possessions. One of the siblings, my aunt, was left out of his will. There was a major question as to what to do with the house, which was located next to a nursing home, Winebrenner Extended Care Facility. They had been trying for years to purchase the house from my grandfather, who refused to sell. Eventually, my mother's older siblings, executors of the estate, sold the house to Winebrenner, who was eager to make an offer now that my grandfather was dead. The facility's plan was to demolish the house and use it for parking and building expansion. My mother and father briefly looked into moving the house, but the cost of transporting an old, two-story home was astronomical.

On an otherwise normal day, we gathered to watch a wrecking crew tear it all down: the house, the apple tree, the garage out back where I once threw a rock and broke a window, just to see what it would feel like. Within a few weeks, not a trace of it remained. My mother's childhood home, and a second home of my own, was no longer there.

two

White Trash Nation

O n April 7, 1994, I turned ten years old. The following day, the body of Kurt Cobain was found at his residence outside Seattle. Although I didn't fully grasp the meaning of his suicide, I was devastated: Cobain had become my childhood idol. My inchoate feelings of inadequacy and alienation had found expression in the popular grunge culture of the time, especially in Cobain's cultivated dirtbag, melancholic image. With permission from my parents, who encouraged me to "express myself," I grew my hair out and wore tattered clothes from the Salvation Army (which worked out well since we got many of our clothes there anyway). I also began skateboarding, spending many hours circling the streets until dark. None of this was unusual among young boys at the time—or young children of other generations, who have had their own icons to look up to and imitate—but, nevertheless, the particular trends of the 1990s, which embraced a post-punk, anti-establishment sentiment, acted as cultural markers that could offer me some semblance of a coherent identity. It gave me something to celebrate, something that laid claim to authenticity and a rejection of the soulless, corporate ethos of shopping malls and mindless pop music.

I was, in a word, defiant. In what would prove to be an enduring pattern, I looked for ways to get in trouble. I began to steal with increasing frequency: first a pack of baseball cards from the discount store, which I felt guilty enough to return the next day, and later food from the school cafeteria, for which I would be disciplined after eventually getting caught. I did this not because my family was too poor to afford small purchases, but rather because the transgression seemed to make intuitive sense. Though I didn't realize it at the time, my father and uncles would also often steal from the local carry-outs and grocery stores—partly for the fun of it (they were usually a bit drunk), and partly, I think, because not having money is easier to accept if you can learn to cheat the system. My father never cared much about money, and, in fact, seemed actively to despise the idea of material possessions, but my uncles wanted to be successful. They were innovative, infected with the capitalist spirit, and had accepted the old creed of "buying cheap and selling dear." If you can get something for free instead of paying for it, they thought, why wouldn't you? Besides, they thought, these stores were marking up stuff to make a buck and ripping off poor people in the process, so they weren't exactly innocent. Such rationalization was common, a story we could tell to make sense of our place in the hierarchy.

My closest friend during this time was a boy named Nathan. He looked older than me, and had darker skin with black hair and very brown eyes, which, in our predominately white school, made him stand out. He claimed to have Native American ancestry, though I was never certain how true this was (my father had also once claimed such ancestry, but it turned out to be family lore). Nathan came from a fatherless home, and his mother was often working. He had an older brother who was tall and thin and always smelled like body odor and cigarettes, and whenever Nathan and I were at the house he liked to rough us around to see if we would cry. Once, he filled a sock with quarters and used it to chase us around and whip us on our arms and legs. "Where you going?" he laughed, a lit cigarette dangling from his lips the entire time.

Nathan was the first friend I wanted to impress. I turned to him for the validation that I would not get from the snobs and future jocks. He liked that I was a white trash kid who wore torn jeans and plaid shirts. Although different in many ways, Nathan and I identified with a similar stigma surrounding white poverty, and poverty generally. Growing up in a mobile home or a poor neighborhood in a small Midwestern city, especially one with a decent amount of money like Findlay, you get used to your life, and your family, being used as a punchline.

That year, *New York* magazine titled its August issue "White Trash Nation." Its cover was a picture of Anna-Nicole Smith with a bag of Cheez Doodles between her legs. Next to her, a list of names and a cheap joke: "Tonya, Lisa Marie, John & Lorena, Roseanne & Tom, Paula & Gennifer & Bill. They're Everywhere. Lock up your Twinkies." The featured essay by Tad Friend, now a writer for the *New Yorker*, made it clear that we had entered the "age of white trash," one which "encapsulates the galloping sleaze that has overrun both rural and urban America." While noting that white trash was loosely tied to the growth of an impoverished underclass, Friend nevertheless dismissed this. "What's alarming," he noted, "is not so much the burgeoning number of people with low-rent circumstances as the exponential spread in stereotypically white-trash behavior, whether exhibited by those in the underclass or by figures like Roseanne Arnold and Bill Clinton." In other words, white-trashiness was a fundamentally cultural matter, and the proof was that both poor and rich, rural and urban, were indulging in its trashy transgressions. Forget class inequality; the real problem was lack of inhibition. Or, as Friend put it, "The boom in trash behavior clearly owes less to Marx than to Freud, less to the resolution of class dialectics than to simple indulgence of the id."

I didn't read that issue of the magazine at the time, but I didn't need to, because I already knew what it said. Hearing wealthier kids around me calling people white trash or hicks or rednecks, often as a taunt, was a way of quickly identifying just what kind of people they saw as beneath them: poor and uncultured, with bad manners and bad habits. Perhaps this is why, instead of attempting to change this perception, Nathan and I embraced it in our own way, as though we could transform our stigma into pride through some kind of alchemy. Deep down, I still yearned to be a kid from a family with money, but this seemed like a nice substitute for the time being. At the very least, it was a way of passing the time until we got lucky somehow.

There is a picture of Nathan and me from that year, sitting together at a football game. I am clad in various shades of denim, my long hair swooped across my forehead, my arm resting on Nathan's shoulder. He is sitting beside me in a black jacket and mud-stained pants, his hair parted down the middle and falling just at his eyes. It is cold outside, maybe late fall or early spring. The trees behind us are naked, their branches puncturing a gray Ohio sky. I don't remember who took the picture, or why we were at the middle school stadium. Most likely, we just wanted something to do, something to kill the time. What is most striking is our expressions: defiant, but somehow happy, smiling like two kids with a secret. We didn't have any big secrets, of course, just a quiet sense of loneliness and isolation, one we managed temporarily to forget when we were together, which we were often.

This wouldn't last long. Within a year or two, Nathan would move away. I would continue trying on identities, as though with the right one, I might finally have a home in the world—as though I might be a somebody rather than anybody at all.

Everything changed, or seemed to change, in the fall of 1995, when my mother and father purchased a new house on the west side of Findlay. It had been owned by the same elderly couple since the 1970s, and although it hadn't been updated in years and needed a lot of work (the interior decorating could only be described as a puke-green and vomit-orange color scheme, with shades of fecal brown), it was almost twice the size of our old home. It was also in an attractive, culturally middle-class neighborhood. The neighborhood kids were no longer the children of factory workers and cashiers but engineers and professors, and it was easy to imagine I belonged to this crowd. Our financial situation had not improved dramatically, but due to shifts in the housing market my mother's business had begun to grow: interest rates had fallen after the recession of 1990–91; housing prices had been declining after a peak in the 1980s; and in 1992, the Federal Housing Enterprising Financial Safety and Soundness Act included an affordable housing provision requiring Freddie Gray and Fannie Mac to lend to underserved (higher risk) borrowers, which they offset by pooling and selling sub-prime mortgages as securities (a major factor in the 2008 crisis). This allowed my parents to save up to afford a down payment, and this home seemed like a good fit. Six years after leaving the trailer in the country, we finally upgraded to something respectable.

I felt as though we had finally made it. In my mind, moving to this house meant that we were practically rich, but my conception of wealth was deeply distorted by my earlier experiences in the trailer park and the house on Terrace Lane: in the broader scheme of things, we were still working class. Our house was certainly more spacious than anything we had ever had, but it was hardly exceptional, and it paled in comparison to some of the mansions and large estates that could be found in the surrounding country, or even the nicer neighborhoods and subdivisions that were expanding on the east side with investments from doctors and lawyers. My worldview was also limited by the fact that I had never been to a major metropolitan city other than Toledo and Columbus, so the million-dollar brownstones and condos of New York City or Chicago, or the exurban estates of the truly wealthy, were inconceivable to me. Our house, and the many similar suburban houses around the neighborhood, were simply as nice as things got.

What we had was also illusory, by which I mean the outward markers of our class status—the house in a subdivision, the car,

the quaint neighborhood—did not meaningfully reflect our true
financial situation. What I didn't know at the time was that my
parents had gotten into trouble with the IRS for failing to file two
years of taxes, and that in addition to this, my mother had begun
to accrue a growing mound of credit card debt (somewhere in the
range of $30,000). Combined with my father's student loans, a
mortgage, and car payments—to say nothing of raising two kids—
whatever income they brought home was quickly siphoned into
various banking and financial institutions. Again, our situation
was not uncommon for many working-class families in the 1990s:
to supplement a dwindling income, many resorted to increased
use of credit cards and other forms of debt to stay afloat. By the
time we moved into our new home in 1995, over a billion credit
cards were being used across the country to cover bills, and also
to purchase convenient household items and luxuries made possible by new technologies.[1] Household debt reached historic highs,
and within a few years—the turn of the century—total household debt in the United States would exceed total household
disposable income by 10 percent.[2]

For the capitalist class, all of this was incredibly beneficial:
not only did stagnating wages mean they were paying employees
less, interest on borrowed debt (especially mortgages) meant they
were making money from the debt that inevitably incurred as a
result of lower wages. As Paul Mattick notes, "the steadily increas-
ing facilitation of consumer debt— from credit-card financing to
easy-to-get mortgages—that helped maintain the level of business
activity was also another means, like inflation, to lower wages by
raising prices: the additional cost of items is collected by financial
institutions under the name of interest."[3] The rich were getting
richer from both sides, in other words, while poor and working-
class families (and certainly many middle-class families as well)
were getting squeezed. The Clinton administration, meanwhile,
made good on its claim that the era of big government was over,
at least in the sense that the old Keynesian approach—or, "tax

and spend," as he called it—was no longer a viable model, which, of course, was another way of saying an unprofitable one for the wealthy. Despite two modest hikes to the minimum wage and a failed attempt to pass universal healthcare in his first term, Clinton made very little effort to help working people during his years in office. He signed into law NAFTA, which was vigorously opposed by unions and most working people, and instituted draconian laws to prop up his "tough on crime" image (these hit poor minorities the hardest). His welfare reform bill, which was framed using the language of dignity—getting people off the "dependency" of welfare and putting them back to work—actually increased the ranks of the working poor, especially women and children. When it was passed in 1996, Clinton's Assistant Secretary of Health and Human Services, Peter Edelman, resigned in protest, later writing that the people the bill was ostensibly helping "will be forced to take a job that leaves them even deeper in poverty."[4]

Clinton did face an oppositional congress led by Newt Gingrich after Democrats lost control of the House for the first time in forty years, but aside from the government shutdown of 1995, Clinton rarely went out of his way to take a principled stance against cuts to social services and tax cuts for the wealthy. Clinton was and always had been a neoliberal, regardless of his hip, saxophone-playing image. Indeed, he strategically used his image to rebrand the Democratic party and make it more appealing to the elusive "soccer mom," and in doing so moved away from the working class in order to reach middle-class suburbanites who supported the Democratic party's stance on social issues such as reproductive rights, but who were generally more conservative on economic issues given their own class position. This was a major betrayal of poor white workers, who had been, for decades, staunch supporters of the Democratic Party and were now being told: there is no home for you here. But at the end of the day, those workers were not funding campaigns. They were not donating thousands of dollars and using their positions of power to hold fundraisers, as many in the wealthier sphere of society were. In many cases, working people weren't even voting. Clinton's support of the African American community was equally strategic: he assumed they would not vote for a racist Republican Party, which allowed him to pay lip service to their concerns even as he was passing legislation that disenfranchised black voters.

Rather than reaching out to disenfranchised workers of any race, the Democratic Party followed the money, and the increasingly powerful tech industry in Silicon Valley proved to be a key ally. One side effect of the party shifting away from unions meant that they relied on other sources of funding, and wealthier liberals stepped in to filled this gap. In the process, their influence on the party line became apparent. The tech industry relied heavily on "market innovations" but also promoted a hip, anti-corporate image that contradicted the conservative stereotype of the wealthy CEO: Steve Jobs in his blue jeans and black turtlenecks, Bill Gates with his frumpy outfits and performative commitment to flying coach class. These men may have been billionaires, but they understood the importance of creativity, of spontaneity and "thinking outside the box." They promoted liberal causes and embraced the powerful forces of technology to solve the world's problems. The working man was an icon of a bygone era. This was a new world, and a new economy. The educated man was now the future: the expert, the genius, the innovator. He was the man of culture and education—the kind of man my father thought he could become after finishing college.

To his dismay, my father discovered he was mistaken. It didn't really matter what he knew, or how smart he was, or what degree he could point to as proof of his qualifications. The job market was dismal, and he found himself in a highly precarious situation. After permanently losing his job at the factory, he had enrolled as a master's student in the English department at Bowling Green

State University, where he very briefly taught composition as a graduate assistant.

He never finished the program. He drank heavily, and at his new home, his marriage was falling apart. A few months after we moved in, my mother finally decided they should separate and asked my father to leave. While they offered a fairly standard explanation for why they were separating, my sister and I would eventually come to realize the real reasons were more complicated and primarily involved my father's alcoholism. My father, who would remain bitter at my mother and most of her family for the next decade, quickly moved into a small apartment across town. I stayed with him usually twice during the week and every other weekend. My sister, who was almost old enough to drive and wanted her independence to spend time with high school friends, rarely stayed with us. So, most of the time it was just my father and me. We would get fast food, a six-pack of beer for him to finish by night's end, and spend the evening watching movies from the nearby video rental.

Weekends with my father were a sharp departure from life with my mother and sister. Although my father seemed old to me at the time, he was only in his mid-thirties, which might explain why he often acted less like a father figure than like a friend. He was much "trashier" than my mother and sister, at least in the sense that he embraced a crude, stereotypically masculine swagger. He swore a lot, made off-color jokes, ate nothing but buffalo wings and pizza, and drank cheap, domestic beers he affectionately referred to as "brewskies." His style was somewhere between "hillbilly" and "70s jock," and usually consisted of cut-off jean shorts and tank tops in the summer (when he wasn't shirtless) and a pair of jeans and a sweater from the Goodwill in the winter. His apartments were in rundown complexes where drug addicts lived or spent their time, and they often showed up at the door asking to use his phone or borrow cash. All of this felt familiar to me, however, even comfortable.

In retrospect, I can see that my father's crude jokes and affable nature functioned as a mask of sorts, a performance he had likely internalized as a young man coming of age in the 1970s while dreaming of making it big as an actor or musician. Deep down, he struggled profoundly with depression and mood swings that his love of alcohol undoubtedly exacerbated. He was also highly intelligent and well read in the history of philosophy and political thought. He had boxes of yellow legal notepads filled with prose (he wrote longhand and was persistently confused by all forms of new technology), and dreamed of publishing a novel. He had stopped writing his letters to the editor by this point, but still looked at the world with a critical eye that sometimes gave him an air of misanthropy.

One of my clearest memories of this time happened on a trip to the grocery store where I would one day work. The Nirvana song "Rape Me" had come on the radio in the car (I always brought my cassette tapes with me), and as I began to sing along with it, my father lowered the volume.

"Do you know what he means?" he asked.

I shrugged. It was a catchy song, and I was less interested in its message than in Kurt Cobain's guttural, affective vocals, which expressed a visceral sense of anger and frustration.

"Obviously there's the one way to interpret it," my father said. "But there's also another way: corporations, raping the land and workers for profit. Stealing what isn't theirs. I really think that's what he's talking about."

As contrived as this dialogue may seem, it was not uncommon. My father was widely known as "a talker," and often broke off into one-sided, meandering political rants. "The words 'liberal' and 'conservative' don't mean anything," he would tell me, lighting a cigarette after finishing a few beers. "Conservatives want to deregulate, or *liberate* the economy. Liberals want to protect the oppressed, or *conserve* other cultures." I didn't understand what any of it meant, and usually just laughed. To me, my father was just a fun drunk having a good time.

It was around this time that my father got a job as a technical writer editing instruction manuals for an electronics company in Michigan. While white-collar in a basic sense, it was hardly lucrative: he was a low-level office worker, essentially, without much by way of job security. His commute was long, and often he would stay for the week in Michigan to avoid having to drive back and forth. When he was back in Ohio, he would pick me up at my mother's house, and we would head straight to the carryout for peanuts, beer, and soda. We would pick up a few movies we hadn't seen and sit in his dimly lit apartment with fattening food. My father would smoke out the window, and I would secretly enjoy the smell until I finally fell asleep. On Sunday afternoon, I would be shuffled back to my mother's house, with its candles and kitsch and all its aesthetic trappings of middle-class aspirations.

My father often drove us to North Baltimore, the small village where he had grown up. He hated it there—he called it "hicksville," and loathed its parochial nature and trailer park culture—but took me to visit his parents, who had a small above-ground pool in their backyard. One weekend, there was a street festival, and during the few hours we wandered around, my father drank as he usually did: heavily. Walking back to the car, I noticed him fumbling with the keys. I didn't think much of it, at least not until we got on the highway. Listening to whatever music was on the radio, I sat silently and looked out ahead me, watching as the car began to veer into the left lane. A semi-truck roared past us, inches away from taking off the driver's side mirror. I looked over at my father, whose eyes behind his sunglasses were nearly closed.

"Dad!" I shouted. "Wake up."

He snapped his head and looked at me. "What is it?" he said, licking his lips and fumbling with the stereo. "I'm fine. We're fine."

By the time I fully settled into middle school, the contradictions that had come to define my understanding of my social status had congealed. I was in some ways closer to the class status I had always wanted, but I still saw myself as poor white trash. During the week, I stayed with my mother in a nice, middle-class neighborhood, and on the weekends I stayed with my working-class, alcoholic father. Plenty of people feel that they have no place in a social hierarchy, especially in those awkward years between middle school and adulthood, when identity is still fluid. But for me, this transitional period was heightened by a pervading sense of alienation I had carried with me since I first recognized my family was poor. It was a kind of stain, one I did not know how to wash away. I continued to embrace certain cultural markers of deviance in my search for something to cover it, or adorn it somehow: I colored my hair and painted my fingernails; I listened to loud, offensive music that promoted a vulgar shock aesthetic. These were not real transgressions—they were marketed to an entire generation of disaffected youths—but to a twelve-year-old, they seemed like an appropriate way of rejecting middle-class values of civility and conformity, which, at the time, was the only frame-work through which I could understand my relationship to the people around me. These were the cultural byproducts of social alienation, the performances that accompany positions of despair: the dissonance of atonal guitars, the grimaced expressions on the face of a screaming musician, the glorification of sex and drugs and anti-Christian imagery. None of this was an attempt to criticize the world so much as it was to burn it down in a proud celebration of being the world's misfit, and of feeling alone. It was palliative, one that felt so necessary as to be mistaken for a cure.[5]

I spent many nights in my early adolescence with kids who already smoked, drank, and had sex. They were twelve, thirteen, fourteen. If I had become an insubordinate teen, they were the "bad" kids that led the way, the kind of kids parents worried might fray the moral fabric of society. Some of them were poor, others were more privileged, but in the eyes of most people, they were all white trash (those who were white, at least). It didn't matter if your mother was a nurse or a secretary, or if, as was the case with one girl, your family came into a considerable amount of wealth and you lived in a nice house. What made you trash was your attitude, the way you spoke and dressed, the kinds of people you chose as your friends. White trash was vulgar, stupid, and horny, and mostly just wanted to find a way to get high. Our group included a few high school boys, and some nights we would crowd into one of their cars and drive out into the country to smoke in the massive darkness. Jammed against a back door, I would take it all in with the curiosity and detachment of a reporter. They intimidated me, in a way, because even though we weren't so different, I could feel myself beginning to distance myself. I admired their carelessness, and their apparent lack of neurotic self-consciousness, but also felt quietly repelled by moments of depravity that I remained too afraid to imitate.

Perhaps it was precisely because I saw myself in them that I wanted, or needed, to imagine that I was better. I still wanted to climb the social hierarchy, even if I claimed to reject its authority for the time being. Looking into the brightly lit face of a young boy taking a drag from a pipe, I wondered if it would ever be possible to cover up the stain of the class into which we had been born, or if it would somehow stay with us forever. I could almost see him, years into the future, the weight of inertia keeping him a poor and unremarkable failure. It didn't matter that class mobility was still part of our ethos: those of us who grew up poor and in the middle of nowhere knew the possibility of a good life was so distant, we might as well not seriously think about it.

I had learned, in other words, to think of class as something natural and given. This was partly because I was young, but also because it was how popular culture presented it. A few years earlier, a remake of *The Beverly Hillbillies* had been produced with Jim Varney starring as Jed Clampett, an overnight millionaire after striking oil. I loved Jim Varney—the *Ernest* films were a regular part of my childhood—and I watched the comedic mishaps of his redneck family as they adjusted to their new fortune. Like many poor kids, I spent many nights fantasizing about coming into sudden wealth, but what this movie taught me was that it didn't matter: we would be the same white-trash simpletons we always were. As Nancy Isenberg notes in her book *White Trash: The 400-year Untold History of Class in America*, "The Clampetts may have bought a mansion in the heart of Hollywood, but they had not moved even one rung on the social ladder. They didn't even try to behave like middle-class Americans."[6] That the Clampetts still "behaved" like hillbillies is precisely the point, and was necessary for the comedy to retain its plausibility. The entire plot was premised on the failure of class mobility, with its conception of class crucially having nothing to do with money or labor. Indeed, the implicit suggestion in the film's repeated gags was that these hillbillies didn't deserve their money, so it was hardly a surprise that they found themselves in such outrageous situations. This same meritocratic hierarchy allowed Keith Olbermann in 2017 to call Sarah Palin and Ted Nugent "trailer trash."[7] People like Palin and Nugent may happen to be millionaires, but this wasn't what counted. They have always belonged to a lower class; they just happened to get lucky, like the Clampetts, along the way.

Rather than being tied to material conditions of labor and wealth—who offers the jobs and who works them, who keeps the profits and who must fight for a raise—class is understood as a matter of attitudes and culture. This is evident in the meritocratic hierarchy tied to education. For the educated elites, and those who yearn to be accepted in this culture, the "white trash" label reaffirms what they deeply believe about themselves: that education is the key to success, and that they are successful—and, crucially, have a better understanding of the world—because they are educated. Anyone who isn't educated, or who doesn't embrace the same beliefs that their education has taught them are correct, is necessarily beneath them. As Thomas Frank writes,

For successful professionals, meritocracy is a beautifully self-serving doctrine, entitling them to all manner of rewards and status, because they are smarter than other people. For people on the receiving end of inequality—for those who have just lost their home, for example, or who are having trouble surviving on the minimum wage, the implications of meritocracy are equally unambiguous. To them this ideology says: forget it. You have no one to blame for your problems but yourself.[8]

Of *course* my white trash friends used racial slurs and skipped class to do drugs and have sex. Their loose morals were proof that they weren't socially educated (which is to say, cultured) enough to reflect upon their beliefs and see them as incorrect. And even though it was possible for them to develop the proper attitude and beliefs—they had the same "opportunities" as everyone else—they appeared somehow resistant: it wasn't because they were poor, or lacked motivation due to prohibitive material conditions, but rather because they didn't make the choice to put in the effort. They were lazy, or worse just "not that smart."[9] So, they were neglected, left to their own devices because they were going to do what they wanted anyway.

This mentality has become especially pronounced in the Democratic Party over the last few decades. Declining profitability across many sectors of the economy helped to encourage the full-throated embrace of the financial and technology sectors, which gradually came to represent a larger share of overall GDP and thus a voter base to be courted.[10] As a result, the traditional demographics of the working class, especially poor white workers, no longer fit into the party's electoral strategy. At the same time, the younger generation of Democratic politicians embraced a softer version of Republican scorn for the poor as losers in the market economy. Democratic voters, many of whom were coming of age after neoliberalism had begun to redefine notions of collective action, embraced a revamped ethos of individualism. Rather than meaningfully engage with people whose ideas seemed backwards or outdated—and attend to the material conditions that produce these ideas— it was much easier simply to write them off as a lost cause, as white-trash fools who are dying off because they can't get their shit together. It was easier to rationalize their place in the hierarchy as a result of who they are, and the choices they have made, rather than examine broader forces at work. When Hillary Clinton referred to Trump supporters as "a basket of deplorables," the insinuation was clear: these people cannot (or will not) be educated. They will not "learn new skills" like tolerance, acceptance, and forgiveness. Their racism and sexism are just parts of who they are.

I was not immune to all of this. Not surprisingly, I was quick to realize that education was my way out. It held the promise of being important, of becoming the kind of person you respect for having bright ideas and interesting insights. Much of this happened by accident: a teacher of mine, who thought my insubordination and acting out was "symptomatic of my intelligence," chose me to participate in a gifted program called REACH. I wasn't being challenged enough, she thought, and having an outlet for my frustration would help. So, once a week I was able to leave class and attend this program with seven other students from my grade. Together, we would solve conceptual world-play games, imagine utopian solutions to society's problems (for one project, we designed a "futuristic" car that ran on batteries, had built-in sensors to brake automatically when it detected a possible collision, and had the ability to parallel park by itself), and take trips to museums to learn about science and history. It was an amazing opportunity—one that should not have been limited to a small number of students. It changed my life, not simply because it put me on a long path towards academia, but because it taught me that learning was not merely something one does for a grade, or a job, or a set of "skills" that can be placed on a resume. Education is not a transaction, and it need not be career-oriented. It is an end in itself.

One of the other kids in the program, the son of Egyptian immigrants, would become a lifelong friend. Overweight and Arab in a mostly white community, Andy was a poster child for teen discomfort and social awkwardness. He was constantly cleaning his thick glasses with his baggy shirts, and during the month of Ramadan he would sit patiently at a cafeteria table and sweep crumbs of food into small piles to distract himself from his hunger. He was immensely funny and intelligent, and despite our different backgrounds, we had a lot in common. We listened to the same music, felt similarly misunderstood by our peers, and expressed our feelings of marginalization with a shared indignation learned from music and films of the time. Andy's older brother, Nady, often joined us as we pulled all-nighters at their house, which was located in one of the wealthier subdivisions in the city. The three of us would spend the majority of the next six years together, cooking frozen pizzas and watching episodes of *The Simpsons* and *The X-Files* or sleuthing the Internet for strange websites and new things we could call our own. We embraced counterculture, still desperate for a semblance of authenticity in a world of commercialization.

Although Andy's family was wealthier than mine (their father worked as a professor at the university), they did not appear or act rich or privileged in any way. Similarly, although my family had been poor for many years and was now moving our way up the income bracket, we did not appear to be struggling, and in some ways, we seemed to be thriving after our move to a nicer home; we did not "look" poor, even if I did still smoke pot and date trailer park girls and get in trouble at school. This distinction did not seem important to me at the time. Relatively cheap commodities and a culture that valued individual expression had made it easy to choose and construct an identity, and how one presented oneself to the world was simply an extension of that. Plenty of wealthy people with liberal leanings had reconciled their comfortable income with a cultured, more tolerant worldview. They were the artists, musicians, and visionaries who were shaping the world, and unlike the rich of the gilded era, they were hip and anti-establishment.[11] At home, listening to music, I imagined what it must have been like: the freedom to say what you wanted, the power to not just be at the top of a hierarchy but imagine that the hierarchy no longer applies to you. One day, I told myself, I would be one of these artists, too.

three

There Is No Such Thing as Society

In 1993, the Mosaic web browser made the Internet easily accessible to the general public for the first time, marking a paradigm shift in the use of the World Wide Web. Netscape's Navigator browser followed in 1994, but both remained popular for only a brief period: by 1996, Microsoft's Internet Explorer and America Online (AOL) dominated the market, and excitement surrounding the future of the Internet led to a wave of new investment. Amazon, Yahoo, Craigslist, and eBay were all founded during this time, along with countless other start-ups hoping to share in the enormous amounts of capital flowing to these ventures. Low interest rates, combined with Clinton's Taxpayer Relief Act of 1997 that lowered taxes on capital gains, fueled speculation and encouraged otherwise-risky investments into start-ups that, in many cases, had barely more than a "dot-com" domain name. That same year, Clinton managed to balance the budget for the first time in decades—in part, with cuts to Medicare totaling $112 billion. Spending, the New Democrats insisted, needed to be "smarter." It was an economic achievement that made his brand of fiscally conservative liberalism enormously popular, even despite articles of impeachment.[1]

This was the beginning of the dot-com bubble. Although it wouldn't last long—it burst rapidly in the latter half of 2000—it allowed many to believe we had indeed entered a "new economy" that was somewhat immune to the old boom-and-bust cycle. Terms such as "growth" and "investment" were intoned as mantras, while an increase in the number of billionaires who got lucky coexisted with the considerably greater number of business failures that hastened the inevitable correction. These were the final years of "peacetime," a brief but exciting era without an immediate foreign adversary (Saddam Hussein had ostensibly been dealt with in 1991, although he never presented an immediate threat to the United States). Capital flowed freely, but workers received very little of the proceeds of investment in the form of benefits or wages. It was asserted that, given the overall boom in investment, money would find its way to their pockets, but most jobs paid very little; many were part time in industries such as retail and food, and with these jobs came scrutiny and a loss of dignity. Educated professionals, meanwhile, saw their incomes rise, a part of the growing income gap between those with a college degree and those without one.

The 1980s had been a decade for the wealthy, but the 1990s were supposed to be different. The new economy would mean greater "opportunities" for everyone—everyone, that is, except the vast majority of the working class, who typically received nothing more than a modest tax refund, good for paying off one of several credit cards, and a floppy disk from AOL encouraging them to get surfing on the World Wide Web and participate in a booming industry that seemed to exist everywhere and nowhere at the same time. In this way, the 1990s were preparation for the twenty-first century, when all that was solid would finally melt into air.

My mother remarried twice during these years, both to men very different from my working-class father.

My first stepfather worked for Intel. Dan was an engineer, or a developer, or something similarly exotic to me at the time, given his proximity to computer hardware and microprocessors.

He lived in Albuquerque—part of New Mexico's Technology Corridor, a concentration of private technology firms that exploited the region's depressed union presence, itself part of the larger Sun Belt region that had been pivotal to Republican electoral strategy after the 1960s.[2] Manufacturing jobs had migrated from the Northeast and Midwest to the South and West, where the more recently industrialized aerospace and defense industries boomed (as well as agriculture, with the help of low-wage migrant workers). Dan had made a living this way, but he had grown up in Ohio and went to high school with my mother in the 1970s. At some point after my father left, he and my mother had reconnected; he soon left Intel for a company in Findlay, and they married quickly. He was a fun, laid-back man who played guitar and smoked cigars, but he was also a savvy businessman who invested in stocks and, according to my mother, had a remarkably valuable portfolio. Politically, he was essentially a libertarian, though I don't think he ever explicitly aligned himself with any political ideology. He was wealthy, at least by our standards, but he didn't live lavishly. Culturally, he was a liberal, a man who liked to party and listen to rock and maybe indulge in recreational drugs. He was, in many ways, the archetype of the middle class, an educated man with an appropriately enlightened worldview who, nevertheless, appreciated the power of the market and the joys of money. Never quite satisfied in his comfort, he yearned for more.

Dan fit in with my mother's family, many of whom enjoyed his laid-back temperament. He had a pop-up camper that he often used in the deserts of New Mexico, and during the summer months, we all went camping at a small, rural campground just north of Kenton on State Route 68. Each of our families rented a small camping plot, and each weekend we would spend our time cooking burgers and hot dogs and swimming in the small lake. I liked it here, in the middle of nowhere. It reminded me of the countryside where I had first learned to love the outdoors, and I liked the simplicity of it, the way the days were structured not around the drudgery of school and work but something slower and less demanding. It was a way of life that seemed, however briefly, to make questions of money irrelevant. Whenever we left, I felt immediately nostalgic for this place. It seemed like a promise, the terms of which I could only feel in brief pangs of homesickness.

My cousins often ran around with a girl named Heather who was about my age, and I looked forward to the weekends when I might be able to clumsily interact with her. This heightened my sense of yearning, as my summers took on the urgency of a boy's naive romantic fantasies, complete with visions of a parochial future together in a small, rural town. She was, almost stereotypically, a blond-haired, blue-eyed cheerleader. Although her family was not wealthy (she was from Dunkirk, where most people were mocked for being hicks or rednecks), she seemed classier and more respectable than the girls I had interacted with until that point. Previously, my crushes and middle-school girlfriends had been poor and lived in trailer parks or rundown houses. They smoked cigarettes and swore. They got into trouble at school and were sexually aggressive, teasing me about my own inexperience. I liked these things about them, mostly because I understood them. With Heather, everything was different: she was shy and more naive, a good Christian who spoke with a rural, almost southern drawl. In retrospect, it is obvious I was searching for another way to assimilate into a more respectable social class. It didn't matter that she was not actually wealthier; it only mattered that she represented a certain *idea* of middle-class prosperity that, despite my mother's own growing success, I still obsessively craved.

Heather and I began talking on the phone during the week when we weren't at the campground. Our conversations were short and awkward, in part because we were young but primarily because we had very little in common. One weekend, my mother dropped me off at the campground and let me stay in the camper alone so I could meet up with Heather. The plan was ill-conceived: it was October, and the campground was mostly empty. Everyone had packed up for the winter, but I was there, a young teen boy wandering the grounds through the rain and fog. I waited for many hours, walking the lonely landscape of dead leaves and branches. In the end, Heather never showed up. I sat in the camper and listened to Shirley Manson on my Discman until I fell asleep in the cold darkness. It was an experience in the complicated arena of desire and relationships, and it ended with a resounding verdict I would carry with me into adulthood: I should stick with girls who were more like me, girls who weren't popular, who lived in the part of town that most people never bothered to visit.

My mother and Dan were married for only a year or so before they separated. Not long after this, my mother began attending a non-denominational church, where she found God and became a born-again Christian. She began requesting (and occasionally requiring) I attend services, which took place in a large auditorium that had carpet, chairs, and drab, incandescent lighting—a stark contrast to the old wooden pews and beautiful light I remembered from the old Catholic church we used to attend. It all felt cheap and uninspiring. The music, especially, was incredibly trite, its chord progressions and lyrics dumbed down to appeal to a "general audience" and mimic something like joy— praise and worship rock music, which wedded a bland, corporate alternative with lyrics that might have been written by a lovesick teenager. My mother, however, found in this place an enormous amount of comfort in the midst of an ugly divorce. With its non-denominational, non-hierarchical structure, this church dismantled her Catholic upbringing: instead of stale ceremony mediated through a hierarchy of surrogates, she was encouraged to have a direct, "personal" relationship with Jesus Christ. What mattered was not what those in charge had to say, but how she felt. There was thus no right or wrong way to worship, and there was no one to judge her for her sins.

I hated this church, and avoided attending at every opportunity. Part of my aversion might have been my distance from religion, a product of my mostly secular upbringing. Despite my mother having been raised Catholic, for most of my childhood, she was only nominally religious. We would attend church a few times a year—on the major holidays—and for a brief period, my sister and I attended catechism, but for the most part, we were not a religious family. My father, a transcendentalist, sometimes spoke of God but always as a substitute for something more vague and secular: nature, the universe, "spirit" or collective consciousness. But as I stood in the audience surrounded by worshippers raising their hands, I couldn't help but feel embarrassed: they were being duped, taken advantage of, all so they could feel a modicum of security and hope.

What I couldn't see at the time was that this was the whole point: in a small city like Findlay, Ohio, where the majority of public spaces were filled with chain restaurants, strip malls, and big-box retail stores, there were few other places for people to gather and have meaningful, engaged conversations. With only 41,000 people living in and around the city—and only 75,000 in all 534 square miles of Hancock County—everyday life could feel incredibly isolating. The city did, however, have over a hundred churches, and these institutions provided a crucial sense of belonging. People congregated, exchanged stories of hardship and joy, and forged new friendships and networks of emotional and financial support (many were brought to specific churches through family and close friends). In a society with a paltry welfare state and exploding inequality, local churches picked up the slack—by organizing charity drives, providing shelter, or simply offering a place people could go for spiritual support. So, it wasn't exactly a surprise that my mother, and everyone else there, didn't mind that their congregation met in some bland auditorium that doubled as a gymnasium, or that the lyrics to their hymn flashed across giant screens: these things weren't what mattered. If you'd asked them, those who looked down on that church (like me) were cynical or elitist. That church served its purpose of providing a space for people to share ideas, and just as it didn't matter how you appeared but how you truly acted in your faith, it didn't matter what the space of the church looked like.

"I am wherever two or more people gather in my name," my mother would say when I made fun of the church's ugly decor. "That's what Jesus said, anyway. He didn't care about nice things. He wasn't materialistic. He overturned the tables at the temple, where the moneychangers were. He didn't like rich people."

"So why give the church money?" I'd say, satisfied with my own sense of righteousness. Like any contrarian, I wasn't interested in truth. I just wanted to piss on the other side as proof of my free-thinking independence. It was another petulant version of trying to rebel against a perceived status quo, one that many still sadly believe is an effective political strategy.

My mother had another reason to attend this church: she had met someone there, in her Christian Singles group. His name was Brock, and he was a reformed man who had found God and got his life together after making some serious mistakes when he was a young man. He was handsome, charming, and, most importantly for my mother, a devout believer. He was also a persuasive conservative, and after they married my mother gradually traded in her liberal views on social issues such as abortion, sexuality and gay marriage, divorce, and premarital sex. Like many Christians, they became culture warriors, battling what they perceived to be the most pressing issues facing our nation. They questioned evolution and its contradiction of scripture, and at one point even insisted that humans literally lived to be eight hundred years old, as the Book of Genesis described. I fought with them frequently, taking increasingly radical positions, often out of spite.

Tellingly, we never fought about class. The so-called "resurgence" of culture wars (they had never really gone away), which had replaced the Soviet threat and nuclear disaster after the end of the Cold War, was amplified by the absence of an organized class politics. While tax cuts and the continued erosion of public services were still fundamental to the conservative strategy, Republicans had much in common with a figure like Bill Clinton, with his draconian welfare reform and repeal of the Glass–Steagall Act. Labor unions, which hadn't been influential in politics in many decades, had weakened to the point of irrelevance. This, combined with declining rates in violent crime and optimism about the future of the new economy, allowed cultural issues to rise to the surface with a new urgency. Driving these issues were, on the one hand, powerful conservative lobbyists and the Christian Right, and the loyal adherents to their ideology such as my mother and stepfather. As Pat Buchanan, whose own campaign rhetoric would later be mirrored in Donald Trump's, said in his now well-known "culture war speech" at the 1992 Republican National Convention, "There is a religious war going on in our country for the soul of America. It is a cultural war, as critical to the kind of nation we will one day be as was the Cold War itself."[3] Fighting Buchanan and the religious Right were members of that new class of educated professionals, many of whom had carved a centrist position (similar to Clinton's) between the social radicalism of the 1960s and the economic conservatism of the 1980s.

"There is no such thing as society," the British Prime Minister Margaret Thatcher had said in 1987. "There are individual men and women and there are families and no government can do anything except through people and people look to themselves first."[4] This reimagining of the state to better protect capital (a lean but robust government that favored competitive markets over a generous social safety net) was not unique to America. Although England maintained a much stronger welfare state, it experienced a similar conservative uprising determined to set free the social bonds of the public and leave nothing standing but a well-protected market. If the personal had become political in the 1960s and '70s, by the '90s, the political was explicitly personal. The family, as Thatcher repeatedly said, was the organizing structure of society, and unsurprisingly, social issues often reflected this. James Dobson's Focus on the Family had risen to prominence in the 1980s as a key institution for Christian conservatives, leading the charge against abortion, homosexuality and non-traditional gender roles, drug use, and the panic surrounding pornography and "explicit content" as attacks on the traditional familial structure. Welfare, while framed as a problem of morally loose, unwed women that created "fatherless children," could not disguise its racial message: when Rush Limbaugh used the term "Welfare Queen" on his radio show, he was certainly not talking about white single mothers.

One way of (incorrectly) thinking about these culture wars—which have continued into today under the umbrellas of "Trumpism" and "The Resistance"—is as a replacement for class warfare: the educated upper class, which embraces liberal values and a more egalitarian approach to how it imagines society, fighting against a backwards (uneducated) lower class that is fundamentally despotic and celebrates familial units. But this isn't quite right. For one thing, it ignores the larger, often contradictory "middle" of America that does not align itself so neatly with either side of the cultural divide (progressive, pro-choice Christians like my mother today; liberals who support stronger immigration laws, and so on). More importantly, it neglects the fact that most of the culture wars are being fought between individuals who belong to essentially the same economic class (they would almost have to be, given how small the capitalist class is). The real difference, then and now, is not an actual class divide, but rather an ideological difference and the competing cultural ideals this difference produces.

Consider the differences between those who are often imagined as being the warriors in these battles, and who are tossed around by politicians and pundits to highlight our country's divisiveness: the stereotypical "coastal elite" and the stereotypical "rural worker." The former is cultured in food and entertainment, has a high level of education, and is most likely a professional with liberal politics; the latter is less educated, prefers a simpler culture that is perhaps less refined, and is most likely a manual or service laborer with conservative politics or a "traditional" worldview. If class is imagined as a matter of culture, these two men are members of a different class, and we know this because the coastal elite will look down on the rural worker. He will presume to know better, and this will fill the rural worker with resentment and anger—at virtually any gathering of conservative politicians, phrases such as "smug elitism" will inevitably make its way into conversation as proof of how "out of touch" liberals are with "ordinary people." But of course, it is entirely possible (and quite common) for these two people to occupy the same position relative to the capitalist class; it's just that the cultural trappings that go into being "classy" obscure this fact. As Walter Benn Michaels puts it, "even if they haven't got much money, people who know the difference between a good Stilton and a bad one may well think of themselves (and be thought of by others) as in some sense superior to people who don't."[5] And while such divisions may exist in some relation to class, imagining these are what *constitute* class ignores how economic inequality is continuously reproduced with ever greater gaps between the haves and have-nots.

In other words, the problem of class inequality is not that some people like nice things and might look down on others for preferring trite or vulgar things (even if this sort of condescension is possible because certain people occupy a position of privilege); the problem of class inequality is that some people own and control the majority of resources (and are extremely wealthy as a result), while many others are forced to occupy a position in a precarious labor force (and lack material security as a result). And if you truly commit to a conception of class as a function of culture, then you have a serious problem for political organization: solidarity across the working class becomes much more complicated as differences in culture *appear*—unreflexively—as differences in class. This kind of divisiveness *is* a problem, but not for reasons of civility or decency. It is because it prevents people from seeing they have more in common as workers than they think they do as private individuals. What we need is a different sort of "divisiveness," namely between workers and bosses, between the entire class of wage laborers and those who deny them a dignified life. Only then do we have real class struggle.

Entering high school, I still had only a dim understanding of class, and had no conception of a broader class struggle. I knew quite well that I benefited indirectly from Findlay's wealthier professionals and the presence of large corporations like Cooper Tire & Rubber and Marathon Oil,[6] the latter of which housed its corporate headquarters downtown: because our high school was the only one in the city, it was generously funded with local taxes, which meant that every kid in the city could get a decent education for free. Some students, generally the poorest, were marshalled into the trade program where they could learn occupational skills such as hairdressing, auto repair, and carpentry. Often plagued by "learning disabilities" or "lack of motivation" that were more likely the result of an impoverished, unstable upbringing, they were treated as essentially unteachable and directed towards a path of wage labor. This is not to denigrate such careers—the world needs these professions, and many in my extended family were proud to make a living in a factory or service job—but the particular disdain that many other students had for their peers in trade programs was indicative of a broader mentality of meritocracy: these poor kids were going where they belonged.

I, too, had fully accepted my place within the social hierarchy, which fell somewhere above the trade school kids and below most everyone else. I wasn't pitied, but I was easily overlooked as a counterculture weirdo who wore secondhand clothes and dyed his hair. I enrolled in electives at school to make art and began playing guitar in a hardcore band—a musical scene Andy and I embraced because it celebrated the sort of formless angst common to teenage kids in rural towns and suburban enclaves.

Added to the litany of usual frustrations—our looks, our feelings of alienation from the cliques and social conventions of our peers—was a fresh source of anger and annoyance: work. As teenage boys who had reached the legal age for employment in Ohio, we both set out to find part-time jobs that would provide us with disposable income. Andy found a job working at a fast-food restaurant that offered Chinese cuisine, while I took a job just down the road at a local supermarket chain bagging groceries. We both made minimum wage, not surprisingly, and although at the time I thought of this work as a miserable means to an end, in retrospect, it was a formative experience that would shape my views in the years that followed, as I moved from one retail and service job to another, never making much more than minimum wage.

Most of the people I worked with at the supermarket were older, in their twenties and thirties (I was fifteen), and they doted on me in an almost-ritualistic manner: they jokingly tried to corrupt me, and often made crude, overt references to sex in conversation. One woman, who knew my father when they were younger, graphically described a sex act she had performed on him. The shift manager, who always stank of cigarettes, would make jokes about the genitals of one of the cashiers he claimed to have slept with a few times. I laughed and pretended to go along with it, in part because I was young and didn't want to seem inexperienced. I thought it was what I was supposed to do. Besides, even if I wanted to speak out, I was only a bag boy. I had no power, and whatever objections I could have articulated using my limited vocabulary would have either been ignored or mocked.

One of the other baggers, Mark, was an older guy—in his thirties, perhaps even forties—who had worked at the store for longer than anyone really knew. Most of the cashiers made fun of him behind his back for being socially awkward and somewhat uncomfortable to be around, often with the added suggestion that he was a pervert of some kind. He looked dopey and kind of odd, like a math kid who had grown up and still tucked his shirts into his khakis, and had a large gap in his front teeth that only added to the caricature of him that they had created. At the heart of their jokes, though, was the fact that Mark still worked the job he did: he had done nothing else with his life, either because he was too stupid or too strange, so now he was stuck working as a pathetic bag boy. Never mind that the people who made fun of him were also older and working in the same supermarket, what mattered is that, to them, they were there only there temporarily, until something better came alone. Mark was there because he had nowhere else to go. I often felt a profound sadness for Mark, one that was, no doubt, a recognition of some injustice I could not yet place: the humiliation of these jobs, the public degradation.

Even for those working in the service industry, a job like ours was something to look down upon as less respectable. Traditional blue-collar work long had a certain masculine honor attached to it, but the service economy is implicitly feminized and, for many, emasculating. It leaves workers feeling powerless and overlooked, as their contribution appears relatively meaningless and their status as low-wage workers often means they see the job as merely a means to an end and are thus alienated from the work they are performing—a mindless "clock-in, clock-out" mentality that only heightens frustration. Unsurprisingly, my coworkers would respond in the only way they knew, with an ironic distance that translated into crude humor and the mocking of someone they could paint as even more miserable than they were. Viewing work through the lens of meritocracy, they implicitly understood our jobs as the work of those whose failures have prevented them from getting a "real job." Stocking shelves, running a cash register, greeting customers—these jobs were for the unambitious.

This kind of work also required a near-constant submissiveness to both management and customers. Without the presence of a union to represent us, the conditions of such employment could be incredibly demoralizing. Aside from being the target of crude humor and mockery, workers were often subject to retribution from management for minor mistakes, which took the form of losing hours, having your schedule changed to inconvenient shifts (all closing or opening shifts, which no one wanted), or verbal abuse. Although the store prided itself on being a smaller, family-oriented competitor to local giants such as Kroger, Walmart, and Meijer, its operations were not unlike that of those faceless corporations. As Barbara Ehrenreich writes in *Nickel and Dimed* (2001), her landmark exploration of low-wage work,

> What surprised and offended me most about the low-wage workplace . . . was the extent to which one is required to surrender one's basic civil rights and—what boils down to the same thing—self-respect.[7]

Ehrenreich lists other indignities, such as routine drug testing (often in the presence of an aide or technician) and petty retribution by management for voicing complaints. Again, without a union for support (or any mechanism for workers to pool their power), management is free to "run the ship" in as tyrannical of a manner as it sees fit. If workers don't like it, they are free to be fired and replaced by someone who won't speak up.

Workers in all industries face the threat of losing their job. This is built into the structure of wage-labor, which ensures that

workers by and large cannot bargain with employers to estab-
lish a higher wage or some form of job security, or to share in
the profits made by those who employ them. That the scen-
ario of a minimum-wage fast-food employee asking for more
money when offered a job would strike many as laughable—even
ungrateful—is a testament to how "natural" this unequal distribution of power appears. In the supposedly "low-skilled" service
industry, this power imbalance is especially pronounced. This,
in turn, has the effect of placing workers in competition with
each other, something that unions aim to contain through the
formation of a shared collectivity and the recognition that the
interests of workers are fundamentally at odds with those of
management. Competition becomes another way to keep wages
low: the knowledge that someone else might be willing to work
for less is great motivation to both accept a lower position and
the conditions that go along with it. Anyone who has struggled
to find work understands the implicit shame attached to this
acceptance, despite the sunny picture that pundits and politicians paint with terms like "choice" and "competition." You
are placed in degrading positions of subservience, and looked
down upon by many who perceive this "career" as the outcome
of bad choices or poor work ethic. On top of it all, you can't
even support yourself on a minimum wage in the way that was
once possible.

Unions were never perfect, of course, and often suffered
from the same hierarchical structures as the workplace. In the
meantime, it is worth remembering that still today not all unions
are created equal: they have the potential to function as a critical component in the creation of class solidarity, but some, such
as police unions, are aligned with institutions that actively work
against the interests of the working class (even if many police
officers belong to the working class). If we are truly to address
the exploitation of wage-labor and restore dignity to the kinds
of work encompassed in this sector, we must eventually move

beyond union organization within a capitalist framework to a far more radical restructuring of economic power.

My father, after having left a unionized job of his own, was becoming less radical as the 1990s came to a close with apocalyptic fears and Y2K hysteria. No longer part of an industry in which collective bargaining encouraged solidarity, he acquiesced into his role as a white-collar grunt. He was pushing forty, after all, and the days of being an idealist seemed to be over. While still generally left-leaning, the passion that filled his letters had, no doubt, given way to disappointment as he settled into an unfulfilling career that was nothing like what he had imagined for himself. He was neither a writer, nor an actor, nor someone important. He was just an office worker. Added to this, he had become a loner, which meant he stopped having the sorts of conversations with friends that fueled his hatred of the ruling class. After work, he went to the gym, drank beer, and spent time with a son whose taste in music he didn't understand and likely made him feel older than he was.

He was also in love again. In the short days just before the new millennium, on Christmas Eve in 1999, my father married a Sicilian American with a name as loud as her personality: Cynara Defrancesco. Born and raised in Queens, she was working-class to the bone. She had moved to Findlay in the early 1990s with her son to offer him a stable life in a slower-paced town. She was a single mom with an autistic brother to look after, and with family in the area it made sense to move to where cost of living was low and her brother could find a home to receive the attention and care he needed. She met my father shortly after he moved out of the house he had recently purchased with my mother, but they had largely kept their relationship a secret. Cynara worked at a drive-thru and sold antiques for a living, but her mother, Starling, who was slowly dying of breast cancer, transferred the title to her home on Lesa Avenue to her. The wedding was held in the living room of that home so Starling could attend, and I served as my father's best man. He insisted I not dress up, so I gave my speech to a group of mostly inebriated friends and relatives in a blue sweater (with painted fingernails, a signature performance of my refusal to "conform" to masculine ideals). Cynara walked down the steps into the living room, and the two were married not far from a Christmas tree adorned with small, puppet-like ornaments Starling had made of a masturbating Michael Jackson and a nearly nude Madonna. It was an appropriately counterculture wedding for a transcendentalist who idolized the book *Zen and the Art of Motorcycle Maintenance* and a woman who seemed to have made it her life's mission to give the finger to bourgeois civility.

Starling died a short time after the wedding, and a year later, my father and Cynara sold the house and moved to the Toledo area where my father got a job in human resources. In the final years of the dot-com bubble, my father had found what seemed to be a decent, salaried position doing what was otherwise easy work. The economy was booming, particularly for the sort of entry-level white-collar jobs he was helping people find. He and Cynara spent many nights partying with a fair amount of liquor and pot, occasionally extending a joint to me or slipping me a screwdriver as long I promised to spend the night and allow Cynara to hide my car keys (my sister had given me her old car, a very used late '80s Honda Civic, when she upgraded to something nicer). They lived sparingly, always in cheap apartment complexes, and owned very little. Occasionally, Cynara would find things while she was thrifting and give them to me or a friend when we stopped by for a visit.

Despite developing and successfully treating the same type of breast cancer her mother had, Cynara remained a heavy smoker. She smoked Roger 100's because they cost the same as regular cigarettes and she could put them out before they reached the filter. "It tastes like shit if you smoke too close to the filter," she always told me. She was an incredibly energetic, loud, crass, and thoughtful woman who told stories of growing up during the Summer of Sam and seeing Pink Floyd perform *Dark Side of the Moon* while tripping on acid. She loved her brother Tommy fiercely, and although his autism had taken his verbal language as a kid, she communicated with him through clocks: each time she saw him, she gave him a clock, which he liked to take apart and destroy. She was a New Yorker who would soon mourn 9/11 in a deeply personal way, and like many, develop a somewhat reactionary stance towards our involvement in the Middle East to make sense of her pain.

Somewhere inside of her, the cancer she once evicted was already beginning to make its way back home. It would take a few years before she and my father received the diagnosis, but when it happened, it would change everything. After a series of unexpected misfortunes and free-market indifference, my father would rage against the world as his wife died, with very little by way of medical assistance. In a tragic irony, he would lose his progressive ideals, hardened by his misfortunes as he slowly became the very person he once so passionately defended in his letters: unemployed, homeless, and demoralized by his destructive alcoholism.

four

The Culture Wars

On the morning of September 11, 2001, I was a senior in high school. When news of the attacks broke, our teachers all stopped class and turned on the televisions that normally broadcast a school news program called "2A Today."[1] We spent the rest of the day moving from class to class in a quiet state of bewilderment, waiting for updates. Most of us were uncertain of how to respond, beyond the sadness and horror provoked by the looping images of the attacks, repeated as if mimetically to reproduce the trauma. Fear, too, made sense, because whatever had happened in New York seemed suddenly possible in any shopping mall or small downtown square in America. At the same time, it all seemed abstract and distant, the idea of terror rather than terror itself. After all, we had come of age in an era that proudly described itself as peaceful and prosperous, an era in which things like this only happened in poorly written blockbuster films indulging in the spectacle of social disintegration. We had been too young really to understand the significance of the Gulf War or the "interventions" in other countries, and, more importantly, they simply were not covered by the media in the same way. As Naomi Klein noted shortly after the attacks,

> On September 11, watching TV replays of buildings exploding over and over again in New York and Washington, I couldn't

stop thinking about all the times media coverage has protected us from similar horrors elsewhere. During the Gulf War, for instance, we didn't see real buildings exploding or people fleeing, we saw a sterile Space Invader battlefield, a bomb's-eye view of concrete targets—there and then gone. Who was in those abstract polygons? We never found out.[2]

Now, it was all much closer to home, both literally and figuratively. We had classmates who were preparing to join the military to pay for college, and some of us, like me, had friends who looked not so different from the men who had orchestrated the attacks.

Fortunately, Andy faced little backlash following the attacks, despite the broader rise in Islamophobia that swept through the country. Nevertheless, he became aware of his marked identity as an Arab American in a way that was not required of him in the past, and over the next year would be increasingly troubled by the developing political climate. We finished our final year of high school and both enrolled at nearby Bowling Green State University, but Andy left after our first semester.

"Nady and I are going to Egypt over Christmas break," he told me.

"That's great," I said. "Are you excited?"

"I don't think you understand," he said. "I'm going to Egypt."

"Yes!" I said. "That's exciting."

I didn't understand: Andy and his brother were not planning on coming back.

Andy's decision to go to a new home, as difficult and frightening as it must have been, was made easier by the fact that he had extended family there to provide a network of support. My whole world was located within the state in which I lived: I had never left the United States, and I could barely conceive of being anywhere outside Ohio. For many kids in rural communities, staying close to home makes sense. It's what you know, and for this reason, it can limit what you imagine for yourself and your possibilities. As a poor kid whose family did not have extensive experience with higher education (my sister had dropped out of community college and moved to Las Vegas, which meant my father was the only one who had finished his college degree, and his choice of school was determined by proximity to his job and his family). I also did not really understand that other, "better" schools were options. Certainly, I was not going to apply to Ivy League schools, despite whatever qualifications I may have had that might have helped. Such schools were never mentioned, and rarely even imagined. I didn't actively think about college that much, except as something I was supposed to do in order to get a job as an art teacher, itself a career I saw as my best option because it promised a relationship to work that was vastly different from the service economy I had known thus far: rather than shameful subservience, teaching was aspirational in its promise of middle-class stability. I don't even remember filling out the application, and I'm almost positive I applied to no schools except for Bowling Green.

I received some Pell grants, but the rest of tuition was covered by student loans. Looking back, it seems naive of me not to have questioned the costs of college, but it did not occur to me that a public university so close to home would cost more than any other form of public education (or, for that matter, anything at all). Again, I had no one in my family, or close to me, with any significant experience. My father had taken out student loans to pay for the last few years of his degree, but by this point, he was living an hour away with Cynara, and I saw them less frequently than before. When I did see him, once every few weeks, he was usually drunk. He had long since given up on offering advice, or really being much of a presence outside of the crude jokes and birthday cards stuffed with cash. But more than anything, it just simply never occurred to me to question the process. I'd repeatedly been told I needed to go to college to get a job, and once I'd been accepted I assumed that was the end of my obligation.

One thing that initially helped keep the costs down is that I lied to the university and claimed I was commuting from home, a believable fiction given that my mother's address was only 20 miles from campus. Instead of paying for room and board, which would have doubled the cost of school, I rented a room in a house with five other guys, all older, and paid for rent with a part-time job. At that point, I had left the supermarket and worked in retail at the Findlay Village Mall, before finally getting a job stocking shelves at Meijer, a regional chain competing against Walmart. It was a unionized job, but the union was not a major presence, and I didn't fully comprehend its function. Our shift leader, a man named Keith, was a petty tyrant who scolded us on a regular basis and effectively ensured that work morale remain low. We frequently stole and damaged products just for the fun of it, thinking these minor acts of transgression were somehow a protest against a stifling, bureaucratic corporation that paid us very little.

The work itself was exhausting and monotonous: cutting open skids of boxes, loading them on carts, pushing them to where they needed to be in the store, unloading the cereal or laundry detergent or boxed pasta onto shelves, and returning to the back room where more skids awaited. Meanwhile, customers frequently unloaded their frustrations onto us as representatives of the store. My body was often bruised and cut, and during my year of employment, I developed a burning disgust for management, whose indifference to and occasional contempt for their lower-level workers only heightened the pervading sense of futility that came with the job. I finally quit, one afternoon, after getting into a shouting match with Keith.

"This is all you've done with your life," I sneered. "You're too stupid to have done anything else."

I gleefully mocked his intelligence and path in life because the cruelty itself seemed to me the point, and because he had spent the better part of the last year making me feel small. But more importantly, I said it because I believed it. I was finally understanding, and embracing, the logic of meritocracy I had for so long resisted. I may have been a college kid with no money, but at least I wasn't white trash anymore. I studied art, read philosophy, and played music. I was becoming a young man of "taste." I was becoming somebody smart.

It is difficult to underestimate the effects of 9/11 on the politicization of identity and culture—especially the tension between white and non-white cultures—in American politics. Racism, of course, had been a fundamental component to both conservative and liberal politics since the country's founding, and remained so in various guises in the centuries following. It had been deeply stitched into the logic of capitalism as the country emerged from the Civil War and the slave economy collapsed, and made its way even into radical labor movements during the twentieth century. The passage of Roosevelt's New Deal relied heavily on southern Democratic states for support and was, for this reason, more beneficial to whites (although minorities did benefit from it). This "Southern strategy" was later utilized by both Goldwater and Nixon to realign the South with the Republican party during the civil rights era. Reagan hardly disguised his racist appeals ("Welfare Queens"), and despite being America's "first black president,"[3] Clinton's policies to combat crime and drugs blatantly targeted minority communities (not to mention Hillary's use of the term "superpredator" to describe black teenage boys). Added to this is a long, complicated legacy of interwhite racism (towards the Irish, Jews, and Eastern Europeans), the genocide and disenfranchisement of Native Americans, anti-Asian racism, the literal imprisonment of Japanese Americans during the Second World War, and the continued exploitation of Mexicans for cheap labor.

The categories of identity and culture are often lumped together with race. While not all identities and cultures are racial, race is nevertheless frequently expressed *through* identity or culture.[4] What we now call "identity politics" emerged as a positive expression in the late 1970s with the Combahee River Collective and was conceived as a radical method for building coalitions among oppressed groups against large, structural forces of oppression.[5] "Culture" became especially prominent in the 1980s and '90s as academics introduced theories of multicultural-ism into the mainstream. Stressing "diversity" over "difference," the discourse of multiculturalism attempted to deconstruct the hierarchy of race, which, by this point, had been generally accepted to be a social construct: rather than different races competing in a vertical, normative field (that is, better or worse, civilized or barbaric), "culture" imagined a non-normative, hori-zontal relation between a plurality of communities. But despite its attempts to avoid essentialism, multiculturalism often fell into the same trap as the discourse of race, for example, concerning questions of cultural appropriation. That is, if culture is what you do and not who you are, it doesn't make sense to say that these practices are limited to certain people who perform them authen-tically—in order to determine who has access to a culture, you must appeal to something about the people performing it, and very quickly you have returned to the same logic of essentialism from which the culture discourse sought to distance itself.

Much more can be said about this specific critique of culture and identity, but others have already done so exhaustively.[6] I mention it because in the aftermath of 9/11, this type of essential-ism was nationalized in the War Against Terror. With his father's Secretary of Defense now his Vice President, George W. Bush revamped American imperialism with what would become dis-astrous wars in Iraq and Afghanistan, the first sustained ground conflicts since Vietnam (not counting the many smaller inva-sions, such as Panama and Iraq under Bush, Sr. and the NATO-led bombings of the former Yugoslavia under Clinton). These wars were, as Chris Harman described them, "military Keynsianism," a way of providing short-term markets for U.S. industry. While this helped the economy recover from the recession of 2001–2, the "high levels of military expenditure soon showed the same negative effects they had shown at the time of the Vietnam War and under the Reagan administrations. They increased economic demand without increasing overall international competitiveness and so caused ballooning trade as well as budget deficits. In addition, it created a new, permanent enemy: Islam."[7] Bush's half-hearted claims of tolerance aside, the rise of terrorist activity as a response to both American military presence and Saddam Hussein's defeat allowed his administration and much of the U.S. media to promote a distorted picture of Islam—and the Arab world broadly—as an inherently barbaric, intolerant, and irrational culture.

Despite my long friendship with Andy, I came dangerously close to believing this picture. In 2004, one of the first videos of the beheading of U.S. contractors in Iraq emerged online, and I downloaded it out of curiosity. War is ugly, I told myself, and I felt a curious duty to see it for what it really was. I had spent many weekends attending marches, and lying down in public spaces to participate in "die-ins" that were meant to symbolize the thousands of lives being taken by American occupation forces in Iraq. But I was not prepared for what I witnessed on that video, which was surprisingly easy to track down on an Internet yet to perfect its algorithms and content moderation. For weeks, I could not erase these images from my mind—the man's terror, his final scream—and briefly I caught a glimpse of conservative disgust: it was easy to imagine that something essential separated me from the men on that tape. Perhaps, I considered, they really were uncivilized and backwards. Not for once did I imagine that the material conditions in which they found themselves—produced largely by foreign interventions such as the one presently destroying their cities and infrastructure—might have helped them rationalize their actions as a necessary response to a global superpower.

It did not help that I had found my way into the New Atheist movement, spearheaded by prominent atheists such as Richard Dawkins, Sam Harris, and Christopher Hitchens (an ex-socialist who had become increasingly conservative since writing his scathing critique of Bill Clinton). While embracing a crude "materialism" that fetishized empirical evidence, it was, in fact, a discourse of profound idealism that gave almost-magical power to "bad ideas" and had little interest in examining the relationship of these ideas to the material conditions from which they emerged. With pithy writing and a smug, shock-value approach, they further stoked fear of Islamic culture by dressing their criticism in the garb of logic and reason and insisting they were merely "confronting bad ideas," of which Islam was the motherlode. Ironically, the New Atheist movement had a great deal in common with the Christian thought it ostensibly opposed, propagating a similar hysteria surrounding Islam and its dangers. For this reason, their critique fit nicely, and profitably, within the culture wars, even as it insisted that religion was essentially a backwards practice that only those too stupid or naive to see it for what it was—a fairytale—could embrace. As Hitchens said in a 2006 lecture on free speech, it could all be explained in the language of crude and irrefutable biological determinism:

> Our problem is this: our pre-frontal lobes are too small, and our adrenalin glands are too big, and our thumb-finger opposition isn't all that it might be, and we're afraid of the dark, and we're afraid to die, and we believe in the truths of holy books that are so stupid and so fabricated that a child can—and all children do, as you can tell by their questions—actually see through them. And I think it should be—religion—treated with ridicule and hatred and contempt.[8]

Hitchens's "materialism" here perfectly illustrates its liberal, idealist underpinnings. There is no conception of broader social conditions, only the individual and the inefficient brain that encourages naive fantasies. Hitchens famously reserved a great deal of contempt for Islam, which he said suffered from "self-hatred, self-righteousness, and self-pity."[9] Dawkins and Harris likewise focused on Islam, with Harris writing the best-seller *The End of Faith: Religion, Terror and the Future of Reason*, which, like much of the New Atheist movement, married a fetish for philosophical detachment with doomsday prophecies about the loss of reasoned discourse.

As a young man yearning to assert myself in the culture wars, and to battle what I perceived to be a cancerous trend of "unreason," this kind of thought was immensely appealing. It gave me an out, a way of washing my hands clean of accusations of snobbery, arrogance, and boorishness: *don't blame me, I'm just pointing out the facts.*[10] I also had a vested interest in this kind of thought and its growing popularity in the booming knowledge economy, which I imagined was my ticket to a privileged life. Like the idealism of the movement itself, I understood ideas as having the power to change history, or at the very least the cultural capital that might be exchanged for money. If I could become the smartest man in the room, I might finally have some power to change my own history.

The post-9/11 landscape of the United States, driven by George W. Bush's presidency and his own image as a plain-spoken "everyman," witnessed the maturation of this discourse as a political tool. For many, Bush's verbal gaffes and perceived vacuity, as well as his professed born-again faith, proved that education set liberals above the less educated, despite simultaneously embracing education as a vehicle for opportunity and upward mobility. Bush himself went to Yale, but he was frequently mocked for being an "average student," suggesting that his lack of intellect contributed to his backwards, conservative thought. But this kind of complacent jab misses the more important thing to note about Bush's education: he had come from an extremely privileged family, which made Yale a much easier "opportunity" than it would have been otherwise. For many in the working class, education had increasingly become less of an opportunity and more of a privilege, either because of its prohibitive costs or, less acknowledged, because not all communities foster an interest in pursuing a degree. Instead, some encourage its members to stay close to home, to take care of family, and to maintain the fragile social and familial bonds that preserve their way of life. They are not interested in pondering the truths revealed in humanities departments; they just want to find a job and be able to provide for their family.

Indeed, today most Americans do not have a college degree—almost 70 percent, in fact. Yet, politicians repeatedly tout the life-altering opportunities an education will provide and are often themselves graduates of prestigious schools. The number of members of Congress holding Ivy League degrees has nearly doubled in the last 25 years (from 6.8 to 12.8 percent), and those having attended private school broadly has increased to 50 percent for Democratic members.[11] Obama's cabinet was filled with Ivy League degrees, with thirteen out of 21 of his appointees having graduated from Harvard or Yale. Meanwhile, the cost of education skyrocketed. In 1985, the average annual cost of a four-year degree from a public university, including tuition, fees, and room and board, was $3,682. By 2015, that cost had reached $18,632,[12] far exceeding inflation. As noted in a report by the Economic Policy Institute, "From the 1981–82 enrollment year to the 2010–11 enrollment year, the cost of a four-year education increased 145 percent for private school and 137 percent for public school. Median family income only increased 17.3 percent from 1981–2010, far below the increases in the cost of education, leaving families and students unable to pay for most colleges and universities in full."[13] Consequently, borrowing money to pay for these expenses in the form of student loans also increased: between 1993 and 2008, the average amount of debt for graduating seniors increased by

68 percent, from \$14,410 to \$24,238.[14] Much of this debt was placed on a younger generation—the children of baby boomers, like me—whose general embrace of liberal social views made them a key demographic for the Democratic Party.

But while Democrats embraced this educated generation, it did very little to help them: instead of demanding increased funding for public universities across the country to offset inflation and allow college to remain (at the very least) an expense that could be reasonably covered with a part-time job, Bill Clinton's administration actively encouraged the acquisition of debt, making it easier for more students to borrow by introducing Direct Federal Student Loans. This was praised as a benefit to those who couldn't afford higher education, but its real effect was a life of servitude to predatory loan agencies. In the name of opportunity and self-improvement, an entire generation began taking out loans with interest rates far higher than mortgages. At the same time, the broader ideology of privatization and the erosion of what might otherwise be called "the public good" demanded a decrease in public education at the state level, forcing many universities to continue hiking costs and thus requiring larger student loans for students who couldn't pay out of pocket (to say nothing of an insidious managerial overhaul of the university hierarchy that saw the replacement of stable, tenured positions with extremely precarious adjuncts and a large, corporate-friendly "staff"). The university had become a new site of exploitation and profit: in addition to workers exchanging their labor for a wage, it added students exchanging money they did not have for a diploma they might or might not use for a career. And in a market saturated with workers, what better way to keep down unemployment than to encourage everyone to take four or five years before entering the labor force?

My father knew this already when he had written his last piece of published writing in the mid-1990s. It appeared in a magazine, the title of which I have been unable to discover. All I have is the page on which it was printed, with an advertisement on the other side. Titled "A Dream Defiled," it detailed his expectations when returning to college, and the subsequent rude awakening that awaited him:

> Follow along closely, I want to tell you a story about a man who thought that a college education owed him a job—a man who could have used some advice from Socrates.
>
> Once upon a time, after five years of brain-dead factory work, a man returned to college. He had grandiose visions of a lucrative career, a new house, extra cash to live comfortably. Motivated by those visions, he toiled nights at the factory and attended school during the day.
>
> He persevered, and after three stressful years of papers, lectures and exams, he graduated—an honors student with an impressive GPA. He was so certain of endless job offers he naively quit his factory job, unaware that the storm of economic recession was gathering. Resumes were mailed. Telephone calls were made. Interviews were held. Several encouraging interviews. On more than one occasion he was confident he would be hired for the job.
>
> You know what happened?
>
> He was unemployed for more than a year. Reluctantly, he tucked his tail between his legs and crawled back to the same factory. He hadn't given up yet, but he did have to feed his wife and two children. More resumes went out, more interviews were held. And more rejections came back. He was beginning to accept his fate on the assembly line when bad turned to worse: It was announced that his factory was a part of a corporate "downsizing." It would be closing in less than a year.
>
> If you haven't guessed, that's my story. I know there are a lot of you out there with similar tales. It's been reported that some 10 million Americans have lost jobs since 1987. Many

of those people had a college education. Judging from the massive job cuts forecasted, the rest of this decade is looking pretty dismal, too.

What's going on here? I slaved away for three years, working six-day weeks and studying, and all I have to show for it is a diploma hanging on the living-room wall and $500 a month in loan payments? Isn't that diploma supposed to guarantee me the "good life?" Haven't I wasted my education if I don't find my career?

No, an education can't promise you a job. No, education doesn't guarantee the good life. Education was never meant for anything but its original intention: to educate and enlighten. If you land a job because of it, consider yourself fortunate. That's a bonus.

Socrates, who defined the "good life" as one given to the cultivation of the soul, once said to the people of ancient Greece, ". . . Aren't you ashamed to care so much to make all the money you can . . . to advance your reputation and prestige . . . while for truth and wisdom and the improvement of your soul you have no care or worry?"

That's what it's all about. Truth and wisdom is what education can promise you if you look hard enough. It's just tough to see it now, because somewhere among technological advance and free-market greed, American education became intertwined with professional careerism. Our culture shifted from one of education for the sake of knowledge to education for the pursuit of profit.

Like most of America, I didn't understand this. First, because I hadn't been taught to understand it—I was in college being trained for the labor force. Second, and this is significant, I was too busy working for the class grades, rather than the knowledge that the grades represent. Besides, with all the time and money I had invested, I felt I was owed a career. Where was my reward?

Returning to the factory humbled me. I understand now that my reward for a college degree is being able to write something like this and feel good about doing it. It's knowing what happens to great nations when they lust for profit rather than pursue wisdom, when they are more concerned with material appearance rather than improving the soul. They cease to be great.

Yes, it is the responsibility of our high schools and colleges to prepare students for the job market. Skilled workers in jobs are critical to sustaining the economy. But more importantly, it is the obligation of these educational institutions to show students that our country is badly in need of repair, and then provide for them some wisdom on how to fix it.

My father was in his mid-thirties when he wrote this. He had a young son and a teenage daughter, and had been married for roughly a decade. Reality had tempered his idealism, but not drastically. He was still a progressive, critical of war and the endless pursuit of profit. He was still dreaming of writing a novel, as well as of landing a job that would allow his children to go to school debt-free.

By 2004, my father's life was not at all as he had hoped it would become. After a few good years living with Cynara, he had found himself laid off from his job in a wave of cost-cutting "tough choices" being made in the aftermath of the early 2000s recession, which had technically ended in 2003 but, as with all recessions, fostered a generalized anxiety concerning market stability. Around the same time, Cynara was diagnosed with the breast cancer that would ultimately kill her. Without insurance, and only a small amount in unemployment, they could hardly afford the medical care Cynara needed. They were also facing eviction from their apartment and decided to cut their losses and move to Pennsylvania to stay with a friend. There, Cynara saw an oncologist who informed her that she needed to begin a treatment of chemotherapy immediately. Cynara, whose own mother had died of breast cancer, was suspicious of chemotherapy and doctors generally: she had watched what it did to her mother, and she wanted a more dignified treatment. Despite my father's pleas, she opted for other forms of care, including radiation.

My father could not find work in the rural area of Pennsylvania where they were staying, and finally took a job as a janitor at McDonald's. His drinking intensified, and he would frequently sneak breaks at work to drink vodka behind the dumpster out back. After a shift of cleaning toilets and mopping floors, my father would stumble into the basement of an old woman's house and continue drinking. Cynara, who by now knew she would likely not survive, refused to put up with his behavior. They fought frequently, and at one point, she left him alone for a week to visit her brothers in New York City.

Alone and suicidal, my father called me one afternoon. We hadn't spoken much since he'd arrived in Pennsylvania. He was usually too drunk and busy caring for Cynara to make the time, and I was young and distracted by the upcoming election, by school and by my own attempts to build for myself something like a social life. Our conversation was strained and punctuated by long periods of awkward silence. I tried asking him about Pennsylvania, but his responses were characteristically evasive.

"It's pretty," he said. "The mountains are nice."

"How's Cynara?"

"She's good. We're good."

My father had always avoided emotional honesty, and frequently responded with dismissive deflections that were impossible to question. "I'm fine," he would always say. It was a performative tic, a knee-jerk response to avoid admitting that his life was far worse than he wanted to recognize.

"The election is coming up," I said. I made it clear that I was hoping for Bush to lose, offering up an easy joke I assumed my father would appreciate.

"I don't know," my father said after a long pause. His words were mashed together, and it occurred to me he was probably drunk. "I think he's doing an alright job. After 9/11 and everything. Saddam's a bad dude."

My father's politics had, it seemed, shifted even further from the radicalism of his youth. Speaking to him on the phone, that day, it was difficult for me to reconcile that image with the man he had become: resigned, almost indifferent to the world around him. Here was a man who wrote critically of the first Bush's decision to go to Iraq and invade Panama, writing that many people died "because of the relentless hypocrisy of our political system, a system that we have allowed to career wildly out of control; a system that no longer exists for the people, but for its own lust for money and power; a system that is more concerned with exerting military might in another country than restoring the environment and properly educating its own people." Somewhere between losing his job to the economy and his wife to cancer, my father had become a reactionary.

I didn't know how to respond. I spent the next few days feeling disappointed, wondering how someone could give up on everything he once believed. But it seemed effortless: giving in to his despair was the easiest thing in the world because, quite simply, it gave him a container into which he could fill his sadness and pain. Beliefs—or having the proper moral outrage—offered him nothing.

All of this was especially confusing because I believed so fiercely in art, in liberalism, in the power of a culture I felt devoted to promoting. I had decided, after two semesters and the start of the Iraq War, that I didn't want to teach high school and would rather be a visual artist. Filled with manufactured nostalgia for bohemian culture and a desire never to work, I imagined this as being a more "critical" way of responding to the world around me. I had been working in photography and printmaking, producing overtly political works that were subsumed wholly into their didactic content: I tore pages from the Bible and printed on them in simple-minded critiques of religious intolerance towards gender and sexual relations; I printed directly onto images of the Bush administration; I photographed gay couples and decaying landscapes. Some of these efforts worked; most did not. But they allowed me to feel as though I had discovered something unavailable to those around me who, like my father, merely accepted reality. It let me express my frustrations with broader social structures that were too opaque to examine—namely, class relations. Despite my disgust for overt displays of wealth and my general assumption that rich people were uninteresting, I did not make any connection between my poverty and their wealth other than a recognition that they had what I wanted, but for the wrong reasons: they wanted money because they wanted to be rich and powerful; I wanted money because I didn't want to think about money, and having money, ironically, was the only way I could imagine being freed from its ceaseless demands. I could also imagine doing "something good" in the form of philanthropy, giving money to the "correct" people and using it for the right causes.

More importantly, I didn't see my father's reactionary politics as, first and foremost, a result of his material conditions. I understood, of course, that he was struggling with the precarious nature of his employment, with his near-homelessness, and with the declining health of his wife. But I would not understand the depths of what he went through until later, and what I did know at the time I could explain by bad luck: my father had simply been dealt a bad hand—and he had, but not for the reasons I imagined. Fate, not our market economy, had decided to make things difficult for him, and that was that. In retrospect, it seems all too obvious that my father's life could have gone much differently had he not lost his job and his health insurance after a downturn in the market, had he not been forced to throw away everything he owned and move into the basement of a woman he didn't even know while pleading with God to save his wife's life.

Bush won the 2004 election, but I don't know if my father even voted. I wouldn't talk to him for at least the next six months until Cynara's son was married in Ohio and the two of them returned briefly for the wedding. Cynara, as usual, did not let on that she was dying, My father, now 44 years old, looked as though he had aged many years: his hair more gray than I had ever seen it, he sucked on a cigarette in the parking lot of the church and gave non-responses when I asked him how he was doing. I lit a cigarette and we stood together in the sunlight, the blustery May winds scattering the smoke into non-existence.

"Pennsylvania must be nice this time of year," I said after a long silence.

My father nodded and looked around for Cynara, as though if he could look at her enough, he might prevent her from disappearing. We went inside, and a few hours after the reception, my father and Cynara drove back to Pennsylvania.

A month or so later, the woman they were living with died of a heart attack on the floor of her home. They heard the collapse and ran up to help her. My father drunkenly pounded on her chest while Cynara gave her mouth-to-mouth. She didn't even make it to the hospital. Her children gave my father and Cynara six weeks to find another place to live. Cynara went to live with a friend. My father, with no money and nowhere else to go, returned home to North Baltimore, Ohio, to stay with his parents.

Cynara did not survive much longer. After returning to Ohio, she lived for a brief time with friends in Tiffin, and then with her son in Columbus. Eventually, she moved to North Baltimore to live in my father's childhood home, sleeping in the same bedroom he slept in as a boy. In the meantime, my father had begun binge drinking on cheap beer. He would occasionally call and ask me for money, which I knew was to buy more alcohol from the carryout. I didn't know to refuse him. I needed to feel like I was "helping," but I didn't have any material resources to do so. It was all borrowed money at this point anyway—like play money—student loans that were beginning to grow larger, like a fungus. I don't even think I registered the fact that I would need to pay it back. It was easy to defer the reality of it for some future that felt as distant as it did unlikely.

One afternoon, I arrived in North Baltimore to find my father sitting out behind his parents' house, nursing a beer. A case of Natural Ice was hidden nearby in the bushes—he thought, or allowed himself to think, he was fooling his parents. I handed him $50, and he took a long drag from his cigarette.

"Thanks," he said. "I'll pay you when I get some money saved up. I sent out some resumes. Got a few interviews lined up."

"Don't worry about it," I said.

"You ever listen to The Doors?" he said and, after a long dramatic pause, added, "This is the strangest life I've ever known." He laughed a little and put his empty can into the case, replacing it with a full one. Then he stood for a minute and looked off into the distance, as if preparing to say something important.

"What doesn't kill you makes you stronger," he said.

It was a moment as surreal as it was disheartening. My father's intelligence and insight, which I had spent the better part of my life admiring, had been reduced to drunken regurgitation of Nietzschean clichés and the pseudo-poetry of Jim Morrison.

My father's drinking tapered off a little as he recognized he didn't have much time left with Cynara. Two months before her death, I drove down to photograph the two of them in a state park nearby. We walked through the park, and she casually smoked a joint to ease the pain. She was remarkably upbeat, and if I didn't know better, I would have never guessed she was sick. She teased my father and offered me a hit from her joint, which I politely declined. We spent the next few hours wandering around as the October sun began to dip behind the trees and set fire to the leaves with its light. I photographed the two of them together, standing defiantly, and after a while, I drove them back to my grandparents' house. My father was talkative and, despite the general sense of impending disaster he wore on his face, seemed happy to have gotten out of the house for a few hours.

"Can you make extra copies of those for me?" he asked.

I agreed, not knowing he would one day spend many drunken hours flipping through them.

I also didn't know, as I watched them walk into the house, that it would be the last time I saw Cynara alive. Her health declined rapidly during the last several months of her life, and to protect me, I think, she shut herself off from the world. She was given morphine to manage the pain, and my father helped give it to her, usually in a spoonful of yogurt. He bathed her and changed her bandages (he would later describe to me in graphic detail what the cancer did to her body, an image he was unable to forget). But he did not want her to die in his parents' home. He wanted her to die in something that was theirs, and after being fortunate enough to get his old job back (the market had bounced in his favor, apparently), he rented an apartment in Toledo, close to his work. He brought Cynara there. I do not know how much she understood what was going on, as the cancer moved its way through her body. But my father wanted to be able to tell her, in whatever way he could: "There is a home for us here."

Cynara died inside that apartment a few weeks after my father pushed her inside on a wheelchair. She had just turned 49.

five

Inheritance

After Cynara's death, my father spent a month binge drinking. His work gave him time off to deal with Cynara's death —they allowed him as much time off as he wanted, with pay— but over the next few weeks, he mostly wandered between the carryout and his apartment. He was almost arrested one night when he kicked out the windows to the main entrance of his building after realizing he had left his keys inside (the cops took pity on him when he began to weep uncontrollably and tell them about Cynara), and on a separate night, his neighbors found him passed out in the snow, nearly frozen, and called an ambulance. He was taken to the hospital and forced to stay overnight because his blood pressure was critically high—he had always had issues with his blood pressure, but this was aggravated by a diet of chili dogs and potato chips. He was also averaging about about twenty to 25 beers a day, blowing through his savings.

A week later, he was back at the hospital. I went to visit him this time, after receiving a call from my aunt telling me my father was "lost." He looked like a madman: his beard long and unkempt, his thinning hair wild. He was skinnier than I had ever seen him, and paced back and forth in small circles around the room like a man planning his escape—and he would, after I left, try to escape out the front door by telling the nurse he wanted a cigarette.

"They can't keep me here," he told me.

And they couldn't: by the next day, he was back to wandering the streets. Eventually, he would stumble into work, confused and unsure of why he was even there, and his boss would trick him into getting into his car by telling him he was going to buy him a pack of cigarettes. Instead, he would take my father to rehab, where he would spend eight days suffering from severe alcohol withdrawal and hallucinating in his room. Insurance would not cover much more than this, however, and my father would be sent home and encouraged to attend Alcoholics Anonymous. He remained sober for a short time, working on what he hoped would be a memoir. The process of writing brought back memories too painful, however, and over Memorial Day weekend he began an astonishing three-month binge that cost him his job (a second time), thousands of dollars, and eviction from his apartment. Facing the prospect of sleeping on the streets, he returned again to live with his parents in North Baltimore.

Here, he passed his days running, sitting in the local public library, and applying for salaried positions he wouldn't get. They would ask, "How do you explain the gap in your employment record?" And my father would say, "My wife was dying," and he would leave out the part about attempting to drink himself to death, about not having a place to live. He would leave out the part about working as a janitor at a fast-food restaurant. In the end, the interviewers would tell him they would get back to him, and a few weeks later, he would receive a letter or an e-mail telling him he was "overqualified," which is to say the company found someone who they could reasonably expect to pay less money for the same work.

"Just dropped an application to a truckwash job for chrissakes," he wrote in his journal. "I've had 7 interviews out of the 20+ companies that have my resume. Nothing."

In the meantime, he was receiving bills for unpaid student loans. Once, while visiting him, he opened one and laughed, shaking his head in disbelief. "Let me just go put this in the filing cabinet," he said with a smirk. He dramatically tore the bill in half and tossed it in the trash, returning to the table with a fresh can of Dr Pepper, his drink of choice during his moments of sobriety. He gave me a knowing smirk, as though I were his accomplice. Perhaps he was attempting to prove to me he still had his humor, or maybe he just realized his young son, who he had spent many years molding in his image, sympathized with the gesture.

"So," he said casually. "What's good?"

During these months, my father's journal slowly grew into a portrait of an unemployed widower with no place to live and nothing to his name but time. He wrote honestly about his grief, about his struggles with addiction, and about his failures.

> I figured on paper the other day I've lived in 19 different places since 1979, the year I graduated high school. Ten different homes—two houses and eight apartments since 1996, the year of my divorce from my first wife. I'm a drifter, a rambling man, forever moving from place to place and job to job.

His writing, which moves between boredom and disbelief, captures a profound sense of alienated detachment felt by so many caught in the machinations of neoliberalism and the precarious way of life it normalizes. Without the ability to imagine a stable future, the present feels curiously out of time: a mindless sequence of events that lacks any coherence, and to which the only plausible responses are either profound anxiety or numb indifference.

I certainly felt this way. Sometime after 9/11, after the start of the Iraq War and the disappointment of Bush's reelection, I began to wonder whether anything could actually be done to change things. It didn't help that I was constantly uncertain about whether or not my father was alive, if he had fallen into another dark binge. At a certain point, it was easier just to toss my hands in the air and, despite feeling outraged by the injustices of the world around me, accept that everything was going to shit. So, I did what I could to pass the time and filled the boredom with something that felt meaningful: create art, make music with friends, read philosophy and literature. I was acquiring knowledge, that ever-elusive and fickle currency that guaranteed some a path to success and others a path to the butt of jokes: what did the philosophy major say to the business major? Would you like fries with that?

At the time, I lived with two guys from the Toledo area, Kevin and Brian. We had lived together my freshman year with a few others, and as we became close, we moved from slumlord house to slumlord house until, eventually, it was just the three of us. They were both two years older, and neither finished college during the time I was there: Brian went sporadically, working in the kitchen of a pizza shop and studying construction management with the hope of making a decent career overseeing development projects; Kevin dropped out and took a job at FedEx loading trucks. He also worked part-time at a small factory nearby that recruited college kids with the promise of a $12 wage, which seemed like a lot of money (most jobs paid $6 or $7 at most). Of course, the job was monotonous and not actually as well paid as it seemed: you "could" make $12 hourly if you worked quickly, as you were paid by the number of parts you constructed and not by the hours you worked (presumably to keep workers from slacking off). Brian and Kevin had been friends since childhood—not unlike Andy and me—but they were different in a lot of ways. Brian was outgoing, a partier who loved to drink, get high, and go to live shows to dance; Kevin was a loner, a pothead who gradually developed stronger addictions, nurturing a genuine fondness for pharmaceuticals. He was introspective and quiet, and spent many hours alone in his room listening to Bob Dylan and watching films.

We spent many nights together, often with varying characters stopping by to join us. I didn't drink alcohol, partly because of my father, so when Brian would leave for the bars or to a party across town, Kevin and I would stay up and smoke cigarettes and watch movies together. He would snort a few lines of something—Adderall, Valium, sometimes cocaine—and we would discuss politics, literature, and music. On nice nights, we would climb onto the roof and watch the drunk college kids stumble downtown to bars, laughing at what seemed to us a foolish ritual. We were slackers, not so much moving through life as allowing life to push us wherever it seemed to want to take us. Ironically, despite the drugs and sometimes agonizing anxiety, Kevin was regularly praised by his company for his performance at work, and even received official recognition for being an outstanding employee. It was not exciting work—he had moved up to being a manager at FedEx—but it was, in its own way, meaningful to him. He appreciated the structure, the responsibility of ensuring things operated smoothly, deriving a sense of purpose from what others might have seen as alienating menial labor.

After quitting my job at the supermarket, I had been working at an independent record store that was regionally renowned. I worked a few days a week, just enough to cover rent and food, and Kevin would often stop by to look for music. My father, too, when he needed to get away from the rural culture of North Baltimore, where the entire downtown area consists of two stop lights and he found solitude only in the local public library, would stop by in search of some album he remembered from his youth. It was and remains the best wage-labor job I have ever worked. As an art student with a deep hatred of work, running the register at a record store presented itself as a better alternative to the monotonous drudgery of office work, the monotony and degradation of the food industry, or monotonous and menial factory work. It was a "cool" job, as those who worked there were privileged by their knowledge of musical subcultures. On the other hand, we made very little money: the owner could not give us competitive wages because he did not have a massive operation to support them. Even if he could have, he didn't need to, given—as he liked to remind us—the stack of resumes on his desk. As for the employees, in the twilight years before the Great Recession, we had already accepted the logic of "doing what you love," that brilliant strategy employed by Apple and other companies to encourage workers to trade material compensation for the ephemerality of things like "exposure," "experience," and "recognition." As Miya Tokumitsu writes:

> In masking the very exploitative mechanisms of labor that it fuels, ["doing what you love"] is, in fact, the most perfect ideological tool of capitalism. It shunts aside the labor of others and disguises our own labor to ourselves. It hides the fact that if we acknowledged all of our work as work, we could set appropriate limits for it, demanding fair compensation and humane schedules that allow for family and leisure time.[1]

In some ways, we were fortunate. Our boss genuinely treated us with respect—becoming a father figure to many of us—and created a fun atmosphere that fostered camaraderie and a sense of belonging. People were quick to cover each other's shifts if someone needed the day off, and we saw ourselves less as coworkers and more as a small community. If we worked until closing at midnight on Friday or Saturday, we were allowed to take money from the cash register and buy any dinner we wanted—a small but meaningful gesture for those of us who, like me, lived on frozen burritos and cheap boxed pasta. But if we could have separated our experience of work from our roles in the hierarchy, we would have seen something different: what all of this amounted to was just a nicer, easier-to-swallow version of the same drudgery one might find at Walmart. Privately, our boss was a great man, but in his position as a capitalist, he was required to act and think like a capitalist. Sure, we got to listen to music and make jokes and generally have fun, but we received no benefits, and many of us were forced to borrow money from our boss to cover monthly bills. Our jobs were also not secure: while we did not work under the threat of termination (many of us worked there for years), we all knew the record industry was dying, that fewer and fewer people were buying music in stores, opting instead for digital copies. As a result, the hours dwindled, with the store closing earlier each year. We put up with the loss of hours, the too-slow and too-small raises in our paychecks, because the promise of cultural capital seemed to wield its own kind of power: we were envied for working there, and this kind of recognition mattered. It was as if we had all decided that we were going to be poor either way, so we might as well have a cool job while we're at it.

And what else could we do? In a college town like Bowling Green, surrounded by miles of rural farmland, there were not a lot of options. If you couldn't find a job at the video rental stores, the music store, or the coffee shops, your options were essentially either the food industry (the town was littered with restaurants willing to pay servers $2 plus tips, as well as fast-food chains), big retail outlets, or one of the smaller factories nearby that thrived on the inexperience and gullibility of college students. No one wanted to work those jobs. We may have been poor and cynical, but whatever dignity we had left we weren't going to squander on a job like that. We left those to the locals—"townies," as we called them, who lived in the shoddy apartment complexes and trailer park near the mall.

Townies. Hillbillies. White trash. In a rural college town that was almost exclusively white, this was how people saw you if you weren't there to get an education and "improve yourself." Otherwise, everyone figured, you wouldn't still be stuck in the middle of nowhere.

Despite my commitment to what I thought were "left" politics, I shared this mentality. I was a culture warrior, after all, with a worldview that recognized certain injustices but often for the wrong reasons. What mattered to me had less to do with material resources than with the ideas and beliefs material resources (or lack thereof) often produce: how you felt about race or sex or religion. Things like "racism" were almost magical in their explanatory power, in part because they required no serious investigation into how they operated. The only thing I needed to know was that I thought differently. The snide remarks about people living in trailer parks didn't bother me, even though I had family members who lived in them. I had succeeded in detaching myself, or imagining I had detached myself, from that part of my past. Making fun of the down-and-out townies was part of the performance: I was the visionary making art and dreaming of a better world; they were the backwards fuck-ups voting red. I loved them the way you love any family member, but I didn't pick them.

But then, at the end of 2006, my father became one of "them" that others likely witnessed with a mixture of pity and disgust: a townie, a mentally deranged local stumbling drunk around town. Impossibly, he had been given his old job in Toledo for a third time, and saved up enough money to get an apartment of his own in Bowling Green, right downtown near the university. Driven by a nostalgia to go home again, he returned to what he described as his "old stomping grounds." Quietly, I expressed concern that living alone in a college town during the holidays—facing the anniversary of his marriage on Christmas Eve, and the anniversary of Cynara's death one month later—was not a good idea. And despite my father's insistence that he was fine, that everything would be fine, it wasn't: he spent that month drinking heavily. He stopped going to work a few days after he arrived and devoted himself instead to the carryout around the corner.

I didn't know, at first, that my father was drinking again. He called me on New Year's Eve and asked if he could stop by, and

I said yes. I was with friends, quietly celebrating a sober holiday. He showed up an hour later, freshly showered but clearly drunk. His words were slurred, the hard consonants rounded off by the numbness of his tongue.

"What's this *ooh la la* shit?" he asked, plopping down on my sofa. We were listening to The Kinks. "Where's the party at?"

"Not here," I said.

He nodded and sat for a moment, quietly. We all ignored him, an odd fixture hunched on a chair in the corner of the room. He was vacant, like a house without any inhabitants. After a few minutes, he stood and, without saying anything, stumbled out of my apartment and out into the street. I watched him stagger up the dark street, his shadow contorted on the wet ground. I shrugged it off, too exhausted to worry about what he might do. If anything, I figured he'd get drunk and call me a few days later to apologize.

He never called. Instead, my grandfather called a few weeks later and asked me to visit my father and maybe talk some sense into him. My grandfather also wanted me to take him some food, if possible, because my aunt had stopped by recently and it seemed he wasn't eating.

As usual, I felt obligated to check on my father. It had become a strange ritual, over the last few years, a kind of performance meant to ensure that everything was as it should be. As I was leaving the computer lab on campus where I had been working on a philosophy paper, my father called me.

"Come over," he said. His voice was completely shot. "I want to show you something."

When I arrived, I could see the yellow lamplight coming through the blinds from outside of his apartment. A blizzard had recently passed through Ohio and the wind whipped torrents of snow across his icy porch. I knocked and a few moments later and my father cracked the door and peered through the small opening, as if worried I might be someone else. "Oh, it's you," he said.

I stepped past him and looked around: hundreds of aluminum cans and glass bottles littered the floor and furniture, along with soiled Taco Bell cartons and packages of Slim Jims; a row of cans on the coffee table had been used as ashtrays, the butts exploding from the mouths like tiny, mangled fingers. I looked back at my father, who brushed some trash from a rocking chair.

"Have a seat." He sat down across from me on the sofa and gestured at the mess. "Like what I've done with the place?"

He laughed, clearly amused with himself. He had spent his life perfecting ironic jokes like this, careful distractions from whatever it was he wanted to ignore—his poverty, his helplessness. I noticed he was wearing the same outfit he had worn when I last saw him a few weeks earlier: faded blue jeans, sneakers, and a leather jacket that would have been nice if it weren't for the cigarette burns all over it.

It became apparent, as my father asked me about graduate schools and made a few more jokes about the apartment, that something wasn't right: he was coughing a lot, sick with what seemed to be the flu or bronchitis. He seemed confused and disoriented. His speech was fragmented, a little slurred, and he began telling me a story that sounded as though he could no longer tell the difference between reality and whatever fantasy he had been acting out in his mind.

"There was a story about me," he said. "In the newspaper. The local paper, I think. Or maybe the college paper. I don't remember. They stopped by the apartment and interviewed me." He offered a proud sort of smile, happy to be recognized at last. "They were looking for the mystery man. The one wandering around town with all the beer."

My father's laughter melted into a coughing fit. He held up his hand and walked to the bathroom to spit into the toilet. It sounded forced, as if he were trying to expel something lodged deep inside himself. When he sauntered back into the room he sat down and lit a cigarette.

I hesitantly suggested he see a doctor.

He shook his head and scoffed, exhaling a cloud of smoke. "I'm fine. Listen," he said. "I got this fancy new device. One of those DVD player things." He began rummaging through a pile of boxes and trash nearby. "You mind doing your old man a favor and hooking it up for me?"

As he stood upright, perhaps to hand the box to me, his body went suddenly stiff. A startled look flashed across his face like a shadow and he fell back, his head slamming against the wall with a loud crack. I jumped in my seat slightly, uncertain of what had happened. It seemed rehearsed, almost: how his eyes lit up, how he stiffened, and then fell. The sound his head made when it hit the wall. It was almost comical, exaggerated. A few seconds later, he sat up and looked around.

"What is it?" he said. "I'm fine."

For the rest of the night, my father and I pretended nothing had happened. We ignored that fall, and his failing health. We ignored everything, because that was what we always did. At one point, I took a photograph of him sitting there on his borrowed sofa, surrounded by all that trash. One of my professors had insisted I capture this, my father's self-destruction. He told me there was something "beautiful" about his madness. I believed this to be true, or wanted to believe it, because admiring the beauty of poverty and despair is easier than trying to change it: the latter requires the end of capitalism as we know it; the former asks only that we feel moved.

Before I left, I offered to come over in the morning and help him clean up the mess. He told me not to worry about it, but we both knew he didn't mean that.

"Be careful driving," he said, plopping down on the sofa.

I opened the door and nodded, letting the cool air seep into his stuffy apartment. My father smirked a little and gestured around at the trash that engulfed him.

"I'll be careful sitting," he said.

Though I didn't know it, that would be the last thing my father ever said to me. The next morning, I returned to my father's apartment to find him passed out on the floor. I cleaned what I could, tossing bottles and cans into garbage bags and hauling them out back. After an hour, I left and walked to campus. A short time later, it's unclear how or when, he fell and hit his head. A subdural hematoma formed between the thin membranes surrounding his brain, and he died almost instantly, crawling to a corner of the room to lie down. He was 46 years old.

Because my father wasn't found for another few days, decomposition had become too advanced for a viewing. "He doesn't look much like the man you knew," one detective told me, but it had been a long time since he looked the way I remembered. We cremated his body, and held a small funeral in North Baltimore. I spent days looking for the article he mentioned, but there was nothing about him in any paper, just a brief, inaccurate article on his death titled "Man Found Dead in Street Due to Fall," and his obituary.

A few weeks later, while visiting his family, my grandfather handed me a wad of money. It felt soft and almost wet, as though at any moment it might begin to fall apart.

"This was in your father's jacket," he said. "The one he was wearing when they found him. I figured you should have it."

My father had left behind very little. His tax return for the year was confiscated by government to put towards his student loan balance, and his car, which had been a persistent source of trouble for him, was taken to a junkyard; it wasn't even worth anything in parts. After loaning my father money I assumed I would never get back, I finally received my inheritance: a few hundred dollars he had kept on him for beer and fast food. I thanked my grandfather and put the money in my pocket.

Later, I kept noticing a familiar smell, the one from my father's apartment: when I brought my hands to my face, they smelled like death.

In the months that followed, I walked idly through life—I don't know how I managed to finish classes, but when I did, I decided I wanted to become a writer. My father had left behind scraps of a book he was writing, a memoir, and I had a romantic fantasy of "finishing it for him." The previous fall, I had applied to a number of programs to pursue an MFA in Creative Writing and was, to my surprise, accepted. I ultimately chose a private liberal arts college, Sarah Lawrence, on the recommendation of professors and other writers. It was extremely expensive—close to $60,000 for two years—but I didn't really think about the money I would be borrowing. After the deaths of my father and Cynara, I wanted more than anything to get away from Ohio and "do something" with my life. I had never been to New York City, and for the first time, I had been given an opportunity, and a reason, to do so. Besides, the money didn't seem real. It was a number on a paper, one that came with an implicit threat: if you don't take this, you can't do what you want to do. Politicians and free-market champions always spoke of education as "an investment," so here I was, investing.

There was also the school's prestige. It was a private school, a rigorous and well-known institution known as a training ground for liberal rich kids and the children of celebrities, most of whom attended for only a short time before dropping out to pursue a lucrative career in acting or music. Well-known literary figures and intellectuals had taught there, and for the hefty cost of admission, it offered the promise of class mobility. This is what the American dream had effectively become: roll the dice and maybe get accepted to a fancy private school, make connections, and then, if you're lucky, use those connections to do something big and important and lucrative. A poor white kid from the middle of nowhere, still yearning to escape the stranglehold of his past, could "make it big." And while this dream was mine, it was hardly unique. Gone were the days of steadily working your way into a comfortable life, settling down with a mortgage payment and a decent job with bene-fits. You either had something to sell, something that everyone wanted, or you competed for what little was left. In the growing knowledge economy, ideas had made the fleeting nature of capital explicit: success seemed to emerge, as if by fiat, from nowhere. Unless, of course, you were already wealthy, in which case success was effectively guaranteed. For everyone else, the ridiculous contest was necessary.

So, I took out the loans. I signed my name and became, at last, a proud student at a prestigious college. I didn't realize, fully, how the debt would follow me in the years to come, from city to city. I understood abstractly that I would have to pay it back, but I didn't know what this would mean in any concrete sense. Besides, those around me insisted it wouldn't be tough. With a graduate degree, they told me, I'd get tenure and make $70,000 a year, easily. I'd sell a book. I believed them because I wanted to, and because I didn't know how to believe anything else.

One of the biggest arguments offered by conservatives for penalizing student-loan borrowers is that they know what they're getting into when they take out the loans. "When I took out a mortgage," they might say, "I knew I'd have to pay that back over thirty years." And while this is true superficially, it papers over the stark differences between the different assets to which the loans are attached. For one thing, mortgages and student loans are structured differently—often dramatically so. Mortgages generally require a down payment, which automatically reduces the principal one is paying off. A portion of student loans *could* be paid in advance in a similar way, but the reality is that most eighteen-year-old students don't have the liquidity to make these payments, and it is certainly not a requirement to take out such loans. Interest rates on mortgages are also generally much lower than those on student loans, which have been steadily increas-ing and, at their lowest, are now just above 5 percent; graduate student loans, which are increasingly common for those seeking professional degrees for an advantage in a crowded job market, have rates at about 6.5 percent.

More importantly, property—housing and land—is a material asset, one that continues to fluctuate in value. Often, it rises in value, especially if you happen to own property in a developing neighborhood, or if you put work into the property and thus raise its resale value. You can also sell your home before the thirty years are up, because after all, it is the bank that owns the house, not you. Education, meanwhile, is not a "material" asset in the same way. Like so much in the knowledge economy, it is ephemeral and only "valuable" if it can be used to secure some other resource, like a salary. It can't be "sold" in any meaningful sense—one cannot, as it were, sell a diploma to someone for the same amount as tuition and fees—and it does not gain value over time. And, unlike other forms of debt, student loans can't be discharged in bankruptcy. Before 1976, it was possible to discharge all student loans in bankruptcy, but as financial institutions became more influential in governmental policy—and the broader rightward shift in economic thought established itself as dogma—bankruptcy codes were slowly changed to make this more difficult. In 2005, under the Bankruptcy Abuse Prevention and Consumer Protection Act, the Bush Administration finally made it impossible to discharge any student loans in bankruptcy, which means that this debt, if not paid, will be carried with borrowers until their death (with the exception of sub-prime mortgages).[2]

All this has played a crucial role in the rationalization of economic inequality, in part by providing evidence for a meritocracy that primarily benefits professional elites. If you want to have a good life, you have to learn the skills employers want you to have, and the way to learn skills is to get a degree. For those lucky enough to have this pay off in the form of a career—generally people who are well connected and already wealthy enough to afford college in the first place—all of this makes sense. For everyone else, you either slave away to pay off your loans or, if you decide a degree isn't worth the risk of massive debt, you take what you can get on the job market. Maybe that's a job with dignity, or maybe it's a service job that doesn't pay enough to cover rent. Either way, the choice is yours, and yours alone.

If I knew then what I know now, it is difficult to say whether I would have, at the age of 23, accepted those loans. Financially, it was the worst decision I could have made, but it also led to a number of experiences that were deeply important and changed my life in ways incommensurable with the sum of money I could call their "value." Such a false dichotomy, which, as a society, we have been conditioned to accept uncritically as the price of business, ignores the profound injustice that anyone should have to make that choice in the first place, let alone young people yearning to pursue a meaningful life. Regardless, I made my choice: I was going to take the leap. I could see no other path for success, for class migration. Again, I only understood "the upper class" through a cultural lens, so it was just about being a member of the educated intellectual elite. I didn't necessarily need money for this, just the performance and cultural signifiers that could allow me to assimilate. The money, I naively assumed, would follow as a result of my proximity—trickle down from those who would accept me as one of their own.

So, the summer after my father's death, I packed up my belongings and moved to New York. I arrived in the middle of August 2007, having secured a room with another writer from the program not far from campus. Fortunately, I would only live here for a few months, working at the campus bookstore part-time to help with my grossly inflated rent. By winter, a position in the department of Student Affairs would open, offering me both free housing and a small stipend for food. Sarah Lawrence College is located just north of the Bronx in Yonkers, at the southern tip of the extremely wealthy area of Westchester county. For weeks, I wandered around the area, into Bronxville, to look at the displays of wealth: the multi-million-dollar homes, the boutique shops, the cobblestone streets that gave the whole area an aura of quaint authenticity, as if to assure the residents that it was not another of the bland, cookie-cutter suburbs dotting the rest of the country's metropolitan areas. It was unique and special—so special, in fact, that it refused to let the MTA trains reach its village, lest the poor and the minorities find their way there. The only way in is by car or the more expensive, and less convenient, Metro North line.

On weekends, I often took this train thirty minutes into Manhattan to stay with my girlfriend at the time. Rachel was an undergraduate student at New York University, where her father was a tenured professor. Like me, she was left-leaning and wanted to be a writer. She was, in many ways, more gifted with language than I was, possessing a brilliant poetic sensibility that seemed innate. Indeed, she embodied all that I wished to become—cultured, intelligent, and artistic. She traveled with her father, and I envied the ease with which she seemed to be able to move through the world.

Looking back, it is obvious that the resentment I felt strained our relationship, and that my own inability to articulate the difference between class and culture sent me on a foolish journey to "prove myself" to a family I perceived as the cultured, coastal elites that had become the face of the new Democratic party. Rachel's father made a hefty sum teaching at a private university, had published several books, and lived in a swanky apartment building in Greenwich Village with an incredible view; my father was a destructive alcoholic who had felt immense shame over raising his children in a trailer park. I often felt that her family looked down on me because I lacked the worldliness and intellectual trappings of their professional middle-class liberalism. More than once, they made a show of teasing me when I failed to use proper grammar—a playful dig that they had likely thought was harmless, but which reaffirmed the fear that I could never be one of them, because they would always discover I did not belong.

Towards the end of our relationship, Rachel began to embrace her Episcopalian upbringing and attend service at an old cathedral on 5th Avenue. I accompanied her, on occasion, but was derisive of her desire for transcendence and grace. I was performing the role of the intellectual, after all, a contrarian atheist who delighted in proving people wrong. Mostly, I was bitter. I remember, one afternoon, standing in her father's apartment and looking out at Manhattan. From this height—we were about thirty floors up—I could see for miles north. I looked at the Empire State Building, and the sprawling network of streets and buildings through which money and capital flowed at a frenetic, exciting pace. Class relations seemed to be literalized, and, for a moment, I felt as though I were occupying the perspective of those with money. It filled me with a mixture of desire and disgust. Such contradictions, invariably, need an outlet, and I found myself becoming increasingly spiteful and even cruel, lashing out at a world I lacked the power to change. I was insatiable in my need to criticize people for what I perceived to be their stupidity and backwardness, as though, by sheer will, I could overcome my inadequacy.

All of this horrified Rachel, whose wisdom and care I had taken advantage of as I continued to struggle with the aftermath of my father's death. "I no longer feel I know who you are," she wrote to me shortly before we separated. "And I sometimes wonder if I met you now would I even like you."

It was a harsh but necessary acknowledgment that I had missed the point. I was focusing my attention on the wrong issues, and it had fostered an aggressively misanthropic worldview. Her father made decent money, yes, but class isn't so much about how much money you have as it is about what you do with your money, and he did not use his to employ people to make products or perform a service he could sell to create more money, exploiting labor in the process. He was certainly privileged, with a wealth of material resources, but class is more than mere privilege—having nice things, making a decent salary, knowing good art from kitsch. Focusing on these matters over-looks how inequality reproduces itself as a seemingly natural occurrence. My petty resentment of my girlfriend's family's wealth and culture often distracted me from the real injustice around me: the millions of service workers struggling to pay rent, the homeless struggling to stay warm in the winter by sleeping on steam vents or sneaking onto trains. These people I knew were suffering, but in my mind, it was the result of an injustice too impossible to fix. I could, however, attack people's beliefs and rail against stupidity, and crucially I could feel good doing so. Such resignation is the mark of the beautiful soul, who exchanges action for conviction and rests assured knowing at least his ideas are correct.

As foolish as this all seems to me now, I was still held captive by culture, and by my own desperation to belong. I developed a routine of walking from Soho to Grand Central Station, zig-zagging across the southern half of Manhattan. I learned to walk quickly and with determination. I memorized the streets, and, like a flaneur, I spent many hours wandering without much direc-tion, absorbing all that I could around me. I wanted to bring it all into me, to make it a part of myself and, in this way, finally feel as though I were at home.

And for a time, it seemed to be working: one of my profes-sors put me in touch with a woman who needed a tutor for her son. He went to an extremely prestigious private high school in the city, but needed help with his English and writing. He was reading classic nineteenth-century literature—Twain, Melville, Hawthorne—and struggled to write adequate critical responses. His grades, his mother insisted, needed to be higher. He was a lacrosse player on track to go to Yale, and frequently wore Yale hoodies as if to signal his allegiance to the brand. His father, he explained, "did something in finance or equity or something." His mother didn't have a job, and spent most of her time "doing social stuff with other wives." They were not a culturally liberal, upper-class family like Rachel's. They were true one-percenters, the first I'd met since leaving Ohio.

The plan was to meet once a week for six weeks. After our first one-hour session, his mother picked him up from the library where we had met and handed me a check. I unfolded it, surprised by an amount that I could only assume was an error: $150. To this day, I still remember the nonchalance in his mother's voice when I asked her if the money was for all of our sessions, a lump sum for my time. To me, it seemed the only plausible explanation for the amount she'd given me. "Oh," she said, shuffling her son into their suv. "That's just for the hour."

She was paying me $150 per hour to help her son get into Yale.

six

Conditions Are Fundamentally Sound

A short time after I moved to New York, the economy finally collapsed beneath the weight of unpaid predatory subprime mortgages and the financial safeguards of collateralized debt obligations (CDOs). The housing bubble had peaked in 2006, but the effects were delayed by the structure of the mortgages in question: many borrowers were offered incredible "teaser rates" for a term of two years, at which point the interest skyrocketed and left the borrower unable to make monthly payments. The tranche system of the CDOs were ostensibly designed to compartmentalize risk, and because mortgages had become one of the safest financial assets few worried that a wave of defaults would happen at a scale large enough to cause problems. Instead, such risk could be insured and used to generate enormous sums of money.

Risky financial speculation and investment had been helped by decades of supply-side policies culminating in Bill Clinton's repeal of the Glass–Steagall bill in 1999, but the overall edifice that made it possible is well known by its more common name, "capitalism." At its core, the crisis was fundamentally a result of the declining rate of profit on global capital, which had been merely papered over in a variety of innovative ways, from technological magic to crisis migration to defense spending, to maintain business as usual. The "real cause" of the crisis, if it makes sense to even point to one, can ultimately be located in the massive disparity between who controls money and who doesn't, the latter comprising a sizeable chunk of the world population, now borrowing far more money than they earn to stay afloat in a world of budget-cutting austerity. Those in control made up that small class of financial actors who would eventually benefit from the crisis in the form of bailouts, consolidations, and lavish bonuses. Whatever fear they may have briefly felt as the stock market plummeted was softened by the realization that they had the leverage to bring the economy to its knees, something no politician would let happen.

As a graduate student, I was somewhat lucky. My job was not tied to the market directly, and thus I did not feel the immediate impact of this event. I was being paid a stipend by the college and receiving student loans, which were never going to disappear: they had become a bubble of their own, and the government would certainly not allow a trillion-dollar revenue source vanish as easily as the debts of major financial institutions deemed "too big to fail." For one thing, the inability to discharge loans benefited not only those collecting the interest but their debt-free children, who faced less competition for positions of power from their less wealthy peers struggling to pay back their exorbitant loan balances. One of Obama's pledges that excited many younger voters was his commitment to tackling the cost of higher education—which he eventually did, sort of, kind of, with restructured payment and forgiveness plans that were certainly a welcome relief but hardly a meaningful solution (for example, hidden in forgiveness programs was the clause that the amount forgiven would be taxed as income, which, for some, meant a hefty bill). Nevertheless, those of us with student loans were pleased Obama acknowledged the issue at all, and took this as a sign he understood the needs of less privileged Americans.

Obama's victory in 2008, for many in my generation, was important for the political excitement it generated. I had voted

in 2004, but with very little enthusiasm: Kerry, the insufferably
dull husband of an heiress, embodied many of the weaknesses
that plagued the Democratic party. Obama, borrowing heavily
from Bill Clinton's 1992 campaign strategy of "change vs more
of the same," positioned himself as more authentic. He was
cautious on the campaign trail, careful to distance himself from
the likes of the old radical Bill Ayers, but he also expressed vague
ideas about "spreading the wealth around" that suggested the
promise of something more ambitious. McCain even used this
to paint Obama as a socialist, hoping the old red-scare tactics
might frighten voters away. But it didn't work, and in the giddy
euphoria that followed his election, it seemed, however briefly,
that things might finally change for working people. Indeed, while
Obama's support has generally been framed in terms of gender
and race (women and African Americans supported him overwhelmingly), he received massive support from those making less
than $50,000—what many colloquially refer to as the working
class. Comprising roughly 37 percent of the total voting population, these voters were inspired by Obama's promise of change
at a time when the largest crisis in a century had indicted the
status quo.

For those invested in the culture wars, as I was still, it helped
that Obama was intelligent, eloquent, and hip, a college professor with a collection of nice suits. After George W. Bush, Obama's
left-leaning ideals and non-Western name horrified a conservative
right still held captive by Islamophobia, all while vindicating the
meritocratic hierarchy that worshipped liberal educated professionals. The broader message from prominent liberals, perfected
after the smooth-talking Rhodes Scholar (Clinton) was replaced
by a bumbling Southerner (Bush), might best be summarized as:
"If only we'd all read more books maybe we wouldn't live in such
a stupid country voting for such stupid politicians."

I accepted this ideology completely. I had become the young
literary man I wanted to be as a white trash kid imagining a better

future for myself. I was cultured, or had learned to speak the right language and signal my allegiance to the proper causes. I read philosophy and poetry and was, I thought, on my way to becoming someone important. Looking back, it is obvious how fragile this image I had constructed actually was, a delusion of grandeur that required a healthy dose of cynicism to maintain its plausibility. The reality is that I was financially worse off than I had ever been, deferring my loan repayments another year and burning through whatever I had left in my savings. While on one level, I knew this, the story I was telling myself proved to be a useful fiction. Deep down, I was still ashamed of my past, and thought that the culture of academia, with its esoteric self-indulgence, would somehow protect me. But when people asked me where I was from, I would tell them, and they would invariably make a joke about the pathetic desolation of the Midwest.

"Ohio?" they'd say with a smirk. "I drove through there once."

"It's flat," I'd say.

"A lot of racism," they'd say.

I'd nod and shrug, as if to say: "What can you do?" As if to say: "That's not my home anymore, not really. It's just where I grew up."

It was my home, however, even if I could not reconcile the two sides of my cultural identity: the white-trash kid from rural Ohio, who grew up eating bologna sandwiches and attending reunions with racist family members, and the liberal intellectual with the "proper" tastes and progressive politics. What I did not yet see was that this division only had purchase if I continued to accept the so-called "rural–urban divide" that lacked any coherent class structure. By papering over the real material conditions that had determined my path in life—the poverty into which I was born, the ongoing financial struggles of my parents, and the accidental opportunities I managed to receive in the course of my public education—I was left afloat in a nebulous sea of cultural allegiance, where identities could be endlessly particular and always constructed anew. The remainder of this equation was wholly personal, an internal battle between two ways of seeing myself, a battle of moral outrage and personal shame. My father, to be sure, was always on the periphery of this battle: he was, at once, the idealist I wanted to be and the failure I worried I might become.

The personal was indeed political, at least in the sense that my cultural identities had become a common way to understand the political divide. It would take me a while before I realized it didn't work the other way: the political is not, or should not be, personal. I had spent most of my life confusing these terms and focusing exclusively on the beliefs of individuals. I wanted people to be smarter, to have the proper *feelings* towards oppressed communities. I wanted people to stop being white trash. What I didn't want, or didn't think to advocate, was substantially changing the larger structures of injustice in which these battles played out, and which certainly determined the sorts of beliefs that were possible. While I had begun to immerse myself in the writings of Marx, I failed to grasp fully the *relational* aspect of class, focusing instead on the more direct displays of inequality that I imagined could be corrected without substantial change. I played the role of revolutionary in conversation (and in my imagination), but I did not seriously question the structures that made class inequality possible. After all, Obama was upper-class, and so were many of the writers and artists I admired. I had always wanted to be an upper-class elite, too. I just wanted to be it in a better, smarter way.

By the summer of 2009, as the fallout from the crisis was still being felt, I was living in Brooklyn and working at a bookstore in Manhattan. It was a gig comparable to my old job at the record store, but I never settled in to it because the job was always designed to be temporary, a cushion to keep me afloat until something better came along: a book deal, a white-collar job in publishing, something respectable. The problem is that with the commute each way, I was working over fifty hours each week, which meant that in my free time, I was generally too exhausted to look for better jobs, let alone devote myself to creative projects. It was a common theme at the store: almost everyone I worked with was like me, disaffected twenty-somethings who had moved to the city with the dream of making it big in whatever industry was relevant to their talents; to support themselves, they took jobs at cool bookstores, only to discover that management exploited their labor with the same indifference as any other retail bosses. It was easier to have a few beers after work to relieve the stress than do what they had come to New York to do. There were exceptions, of course, but in the end, the store mostly drained people of energy and kept them there, often for years. The regular presence of celebrities added an aura of prestige to the work, but like any service job, it was underpaid and grueling in its repetition. Management had been turning the store into a more corporatized version of what it had once been, emphasizing merchandise (which had a higher profit margin) over books and stricter guidelines for customer service.

Eventually, I left and took a part-time job at a smaller bookstore in the Cobble Hill neighborhood of Brooklyn. To supplement my income, I began working as the personal assistant to a well-known poet who lived nearby. We had met a year earlier when I introduced him at a reading, and afterwards, we developed a close friendship. He was preparing for the publication of his new book and asked me to help him with a variety of tasks often unrelated to his writing. It was busy work, mostly, and much of it felt like charity, as though he felt bad for me and decided to hire me to do whatever he didn't feel like doing. I would organize his e-mails or watch his young daughter for a few hours while he and his wife, a well-known actress, went to some event with other big names in film or publishing. When it was time for me to leave, he would hand me a wad of cash or write me a check, enough to cover a bill or buy groceries with a little less worry. Over time, he became a kind of father figure: feeding me, giving me old clothes he didn't want, taking me to his house upstate for the weekend. He introduced me to other literary figures and agents, and for a brief period, it seemed impossibly close to the life I'd always imagined. I had made a massively risky investment in attending a private school, its cost rationalized by its reputation and the elusive promise of "connections." In the end, such connections hedged on the accumulation of a fickle social capital—a way of branding one's self as being a part of a scene—but they rarely offered more than a gig economy wage. Apps like Uber had yet to hit the market, but the logic was already there, waiting to be materialized: contract work, getting paid low wages but always with the suggestion that it could lead to something stable.

As it turned out, my gig as a personal assistant was just as precarious. Despite being put in touch with a powerful agent, largely with the recommendation of the poet, nothing happened with my writing. After the poet's book was published, he no longer needed my help and stopped offering me work. Not long after this, I was unceremoniously "taken off the schedule" from my job at the bookstore and became officially unemployed. I made many attempts to find work, hoping someone would know someone who might be able to get me an interview for one of the many low-wage white-collar jobs that seemed to be my only option. Pretty quickly, it became apparent that finding a job would be more complicated and time-consuming than I had the resources for, and as a fairly unremarkable job candidate on paper—I had little work experience in the city, and did not have an exceptional academic pedigree compared to many of my peers—I was certain to be tossed aside. More importantly, I didn't have the savings to pay my bills while I waited for potential employers to get back to me. I managed to defer my student loans, claiming financial hardship, and while this offered me the ability to forget about them for a little while, the reality was always there, looming on the horizon.

I was living on borrowed time and borrowed money, piling on more debt at bars where I went to feel less alone. Anxiety, depression, and frustration were the organizing forces of my day-to-day existence. It felt totalizing, as though my financial insecurity had swallowed up the world around me.

I decided to return to Ohio—temporarily, until I saved up enough money to move back. In fact, I didn't have much of a choice: it was very likely I would have been unable to afford to stay in New York, in which case I would have had nowhere to live. Before I left, I wandered up to the roof where I often went to smoke and looked out at the Manhattan skyline, of which I had a perfect view from my building. I could see the giant Citi building, and imagined its destruction, its cinematic collapse into rubble. It felt good to imagine this, but also foolish and contrived. There was a strong sense that everything seemed to be falling apart, complete with Hollywood visions of revolution, and yet nothing seemed to be changing. Our economy had been crushed by the worst crisis in almost a century but no one wanted to question whether any of it was sustainable. Many prominent economists were happily declaring that the worst of the crisis was over. Conditions, they insisted, were fundamentally sound. Pointing to the numbers, to whatever abstract set of data that somehow represented the toil and suffering of millions of people, they insisted that things were looking up. It was all returning to normal. And although they meant it in a different way, they wouldn't be wrong.

As I paced around the roof, I noticed someone else, getting high: a neighbor, a young Polish guy in his early twenties who lived the floor below me. We exchanged looks, and I held up my hand.

"Just having a cigarette," I said.

He took a deep hit from the pipe and smirked. "Well," he said, exhaling a thick cloud of smoke. "Don't jump."

You can't go home again. Thomas Wolfe's phrase has escaped from the text in which it appears, the novel to which it gives its name, and become a popular idiom of its own. It embodies a contradiction, the melancholy acceptance that we must only go forward into ever new historical conditions and the stubborn insistence that people can, nevertheless, find their way back to old ones. For me, it would become a way of articulating my own perceived failures, and the terrifying uncertainty of whatever awaited me in a future for which I had not planned.

I also literally could not go home again: any home I once knew now belonged to someone else. Like my father before his death, my mother had moved many times in the years since I had left Ohio. Her third marriage—to the man she had met in church—had ended badly. He was abusive, and included in his list of manipulative acts was convincing my mother to cash in life-insurance policies she had taken out for my sister and me when we were young. She had been hoping to use these in lieu of retirement, but he chastised her, insisting it was his responsibility to take care of her. Now, having filed for bankruptcy, she needed them more than ever. Forced to sell the home she had bought with my father, she had rented a few different places, and then lived temporarily with my sister and brother-in-law, a musician who grew up in West Virginia and became a ward of the state as a young teenager after his parents died. My mother's current place was rented from her niece, who had bought a new house but had been unable to sell her old one in the current economic climate. It was a small home on the north end of Findlay, and the plan was for me to live there temporarily until I found work and some other place to live.

Finding a job didn't seem like a real possibility, at least not anywhere nearby. For one thing, I didn't have a car, and the city had no form of public transportation. But even if I had had a car, or could borrow one from a relative, the local economy offered few possibilities. I could, perhaps, have gotten a job waiting tables, but aside from this, my most likely option was a part-time job paying minimum wage to stand at a cash register. Directly across the street from my mother's home was a small strip mall that held a discount store and gym. Around the corner, houses were being demolished to build a second, nearly identical discount store. These were common in the area, and increasingly busy—why pay workers more when you can sell to them for less? Walking inside one day, it felt oddly comforting, despite my disgust at everything it represented. I had grown up shopping at stores like this, many of which had since gone out of business after Walmart took control of the local market. They seemed to be popping up everywhere now, and the off-brand (store-version) names were as familiar as they were laughable.

The economy was currently on a slow path towards "recovery," but despite the stimulus package, it was still volatile (unlike the response to the Great Depression, the Emergency Economic Stabilization Act of 2008 did not focus on a jobs program but on the debt held by financial institutions, while the American Recovery and Reinvestment Act of 2009 focused primarily on keeping existing jobs and even included tax cuts). I returned to Ohio a few weeks after the "flash crash," a temporary panic in early May 2010 produced by a sudden collapse in stock indexes. It lasted only 36 minutes, but in that time, a trillion dollars vanished and (mostly) returned. The story was over as quickly as it started, and a later report to the u.s. Securities and Exchange Commission (sec) and the Commodity Futures Trading Commission (cftc) concluded that the cause of this panic was a "broadly negative market sentiment" beginning with the news about the sovereign debt crisis in Greece. "At that time," the report states,

> the number of volatility pauses, also known as Liquidity Replenishment Points ("lrps"), triggered on the New York Stock Exchange ("nyse") in individual equities listed and traded on that exchange began to substantially increase above average levels.

By 2:30 p.m., the s&p 500 volatility index ("vix") was up 22.5 percent from the opening level, yields of ten-year Treasuries fell as investors engaged in a "flight to quality," and selling pressure had pushed the Dow Jones Industrial Average ("djia") down about 2.5%.

Two minutes later,

against this backdrop of unusually high volatility and thinning liquidity, a large fundamental trader (a mutual fund complex) initiated a sell program to sell a total of 75,000 EMini contracts (valued at approximately $4.1 billion) as a hedge to an existing equity position.[1]

It was this sale that tipped the scales and opened a brief abyss into which a large sum of money fell, and out of which it was reborn.

I mention this because the broader conversation about the recent financial crisis, outside those inclined towards a Marxist critique, focused on buzzwords such as "derivatives" and "collateralized debt obligations." These highly jargonized terms worked both to deflect blame (it was not the core logic of capitalism itself, but rather a new iteration of financial speculation) and ensure that it was all too complicated for anyone but experts to understand. What's more, it all sounded totally divorced from the day-to-day functioning of the economy, a specialized corner of Wall Street that seemed to have little effect on the lives of those on Main Street. Materially, this was simply not true. The value of derivatives and other financial instruments just prior to the crash, many of which were tied directly to mortgages and other debt, was in the tens of trillions of dollars, a staggering figure that helped precipitate the crisis. Between 1997 and 2006, American house prices had increased 124 percent, while household debt as a percentage of disposable income had grown to 127 percent from

77 percent in 1990.[2] Overall, household debt had grown from $705 billion per year in 1970 to $14.5 trillion per year in 2008, largely the result of mortgages and credit cards.[3] Foreclosures began to rise rapidly after 2005, particularly the riskier subprime mortgages that had assumed a major portion of all mortgages and were generally geared towards low-income communities. Defaulted payments set into motion the catastrophic chain of events that led to the collapse of the mortgage industry, including the large-scale devaluing of property.

These foreclosures hit rural communities like Findlay and its surrounding counties harder than their suburban and urban counterparts, despite rural communities making up a smaller portion of the overall housing market. According to the Department of Agriculture, rural communities had the highest rates of subprime lending at 35 percent—compared to the 29 percent national average—making them far more likely to default on their payments. In Ohio, the counties of Muskingum and Hardin—only a short drive from North Baltimore, where my father spent his final months—had subprime lending at over 40 percent, among the nation's highest. Over a dozen other counties in Ohio likewise had subprime lending percentages at over 30 percent.[4] By July 2010, Obama signed into law the Dodd–Frank Act, which he praised as the "strongest consumer financial protections in history," something that would promote "transparency, consistency, accountability, and fairness." It was, of course, meant to prevent the sorts of actions that had gotten us into this mess, but it was a lukewarm bill with details that few seemed to agree upon. More importantly, for those who had lost everything, it was far too little and far too late.

I witnessed the foreclosure crisis up close. My mother, still a realtor despite repeated attempts to find something better, had been asked by many banks in the area to handle the properties they had purchased after owners had defaulted. It was high-volume realty, hardly ideal but sufficient given her own precarious financial status (she was now making considerably less than she had been in the late 1990s and early 2000s). Countless homes stood empty throughout the region, haunted shells of stability and prosperity. In many cases, people would leave things behind: clothes, toys, furniture. It was as if they had left in a hurry, or come home in the midst of a robbery, and this was all that remained. Other people took things with them when they left: copper, piping, any material that might be valuable to sell. They would leave the place in disarray as a middle finger to the bank who they saw as their enemy.

My mother often asked me to join her when inspecting these houses, in part to take photographs and assist in writing up listings. Walking through them, I felt like a voyeur. Empty bedrooms and trashed living rooms functioned as a decaying elegy to a life that could have been lived. My mother and I were like archaeologists of despair, digging through the rubble. I couldn't help but wonder where these families went after leaving. In an area without many homeless shelters and a small rental market, there weren't many options available. In more densely populated areas, the rental markets were larger and confined to a smaller geographical space (and comprised a smaller portion of risky lending). In New York, for example, this actually helped to increase property values in the aftermath of the crisis. Real estate prices were, according the *New York Times*, "unlikely to drop as much as they have in other parts of the nation because the market is filled with co-op owners who have more equity in their properties and because there is a limited supply of apartments in New York City."[5] In rural areas, meanwhile, there was simply nowhere to go—with the exception, perhaps, of campgrounds and vehicles, or, if you were fortunate enough, the spare bedroom of a relative or friend. There is a reason homeless communities exist primarily in cities, and why outside densely populated areas, the homeless population is much smaller and rarely visible: there is no home for them there.[6]

This is what made the rates of predatory lending in rural communities especially appalling. Without access to a rental market—often, there is not even a small rental market—home ownership is a necessity. Added to this, more than a quarter of all senior citizens live in rural areas and small towns, and the structural precariousness of renting—yearly increases in rent, as well as the possibility that one can be legally forced to leave after the lease is up—would simply not be sustainable.[7] While social security and retirement funds offer some safety net, they are less useful for paying inflated rental prices, and with the continued attack on entitlements to battle a deficit caused by military spending and tax cuts for the rich, the elderly and disabled are left on their own. But even for those who are younger, buying a home is a necessity. If you have grown up in a rural part of the country, imagining a life outside this area can be complicated. The primary motivation for leaving is often financial—say, a better job and access to better institutions such as schools. But to do this requires either having a job already lined up or enough savings to move away from your family, who provide a crucial emotional and financial safety net, and into a new community. While this is not impossible, it is not common, as it requires both a great deal of time to travel to look for jobs (again, only possible if one has a reliable car) and the benefit of a well-paying job that would provide decent savings.

In short, to leave rural America, you often have to be already successful enough to leave. For those entrenched in poverty, there are no bootstraps they can use to pull themselves out. Assistance to rural communities, to make things more difficult, has declined dramatically in the years since the crisis. As Gillian White noted in *The Atlantic*,

> funds for rural housing provided by the USDA via the 502 Direct Loan program—one of the government-aid programs for purchasing or rehabilitating homes in rural areas, cited by

several people as a resource for very-low-income residents—
have decreased over the past few years, dropping from about
$2.1 billion in 2010 to around $828 million in 2013.[8]

For those living in rural America, this abandonment has been
felt profoundly, both economically and politically. Its material effects have been devastating, as billions of tax dollars are
funneled to the wealthiest Americans and corporations that
helped cause the financial crisis while funding for programs
many rural Americans rely upon disappears in the name of belt-
tightening budget cuts. This is not a "cultural" problem, despite
the way rural America is portrayed as the breeding ground for
everything from inbreeding to right-wing extremism. Devastated
rural communities are not suffering because they are too stupid
and backward to lift themselves out of poverty and "move
somewhere better." This is not why they have limited access
to libraries and schools, and it is not why they frequently lack
decent cell phone and Internet service (a structural deficit that
often compounds lack of access to things such as education and
health care). It is because our economic system has discarded
them to maximize profit, and because our political system has
discarded the concerns of the Americans who find themselves in
poverty as a result.

At one of the abandoned houses my mother and I walked
through, I was reminded of my father's last apartment. The house
had been trashed: the carpet destroyed, pieces of furniture left
behind. Actual garbage was strewn across the floor, and mold was
beginning to spread across the ceiling. It had been easy to understand the destruction my father caused as the logical outcome of
his alcoholism and grief. He was "sick," as I had been told, and
the material devastation that surrounded him could be justified
as a reflection of his inner turmoil. But what about the family
who lived in this house? Presumably, they hadn't taken the same
course of action as my father, and yet the results looked almost

identical. What justification could we use to explain this? What story would help us accept it?

Before we separated, Rachel had told me she thought of those our society discards—the homeless, the mentally ill—as embodying its contradictions: they "absorb" our problems, as it were, and in this way, contain them. Like the fable of the Sin Eater, who baked the town's sins into bread and ate it, the worst among us suffer so that the rest of us don't have to. They are the truth of capital's exploitation. It made sense to me, at the time, to think of my father this way. He was a kind of anti-hero, a drunken Virgil showing me what I might become if I weren't careful, if I drank too much or made the wrong choices. I could believe this because I was certain I wouldn't become like my father, that whatever had happened to him wouldn't happen to me. And yet, here in these empty homes was evidence that it could happen to anyone. None of us, really, are that far away.

seven

Deaths of Despair

G oing back home to Ohio would eventually change everything. Here, surrounded by the devastation of the foreclosure crisis and the struggles of family and friends, I began slowly to rethink what I had believed for so long about culture, about education, and about politics. It was here, as an unemployed, idealistic writer with $135,000 in student loans, that it became apparent that whatever I felt about the people around me, and whatever they felt about me, wasn't going to change our material conditions. Those feelings had worked mainly to separate us, and to keep us from seeing that, in more ways than we recognized, we belonged to the same struggle: a fight for the freedom to live without fear of destitution, which is to say freedom not simply to be left to "choose" how to live (as libertarian and market-loving conservatives insist) but to possess the material resources to actualize this life. To actualize this life, of course, would mean radically altering our world, beginning with the redistribution of those very material resources in question.

I did not realize any of this at first because, as I have said, my understanding of class was still limited to cultural markers. But also, like many people struggling to find the semblance of a meaningful, dignified life in a political climate of austerity, I was distracted. I felt hopeless and angry. After all, I had made the leap to New York, to an institution that cost me a substantial sum of money; and yet here I was, sleeping in the bedroom of a small house my mother was renting to save money after financial ruin and a traumatic relationship. I had some success as a writer, publishing a few stories and receiving modest fellowships, but none of this amounted to much materially. They were lines on a resume, bragging rights that meant nothing in a small town with only one bookstore that few people ever visited. All around me, there seemed only the reassurance that what you wanted you would never get, that to dream was naive and irresponsible, and that you should instead resign yourself to reality. This was your life, with all its disappointment.

I spent my days helping my mother with odd jobs and babysitting my sister's two daughters, both of whom she and her husband had adopted from the state of West Virginia (their birth mother struggled with a methadone addiction). After years of drifting herself, my sister was going back to school to be a nurse, something she soon discovered she loved. I was hardly surprised by this decision, recalling with amusement her fascination with the surgery channel on television when we were kids and her strange desire to pull my teeth out whenever they were loose. Mostly, I was glad she had found a life that was less precarious than the one she had been living for so long—but only slightly, as she, too, would find herself plagued by student loans on top of a mortgage and the costs of raising two daughters.

Most of my friends had moved away from Ohio, as I had done. The only person I knew still in the area was Gabe, a high school friend I had kept in touch with off and on over the years. Like me, Gabe was unemployed, though this was primarily because of his cystic fibrosis. At 28, he had already lived longer than the doctors had predicted, and although he had been diligent with his medications and breathing treatments, his health was rapidly declining. In high school, he had used his declining health as an excuse to live recklessly, figuring that if he were going to die soon anyway, he might as well have fun in the process. He drove an old station wagon, at the time, and kept a baseball bat inside that he would use to beat on the side of the car while he was driving. Now, his youthful vitality had been replaced by something more resigned. He seemed to be slowly disappearing, becoming a little more ashen with each week as his heart and lungs struggled to circulate oxygen throughout his frail body.

Gabe had channeled all his energy into his education, which became a source of camaraderie between us as we developed a deep friendship. We had countless conversations about politics and culture, and he taught me many things, from the history of Peronism in Argentina to the complicated metaphysics of Star Trek. He was one of the smartest people I had ever known, with degrees in political science and Asian studies and a collection of books that looked like they would take a lifetime to read. In fact, he had read them all, it seemed: from Vonnegut to Proust, Woolf to Celine, Tocqueville to Marx, he was a walking encyclopedia. During the Bush years, he had embraced a strand of far-right politics and frequently joked about fascism. He, too, was a culture warrior, but had found an outlet for his anger and frustration in authoritarian politics, insisting that the "natural stupidity" of humanity could only be contained by brute force. In the years following, he had flipped: after getting accepted to law school and channeling his outrage towards the healthcare industry, he had become critical of the market's influence on public policy and the ways corporate interests shape laws. Once he passed the Ohio bar, he decided, he was going to focus his energy on the healthcare system and, more fiercely, the pharmaceutical industry that had fleeced him and others because demand for life-saving drugs is almost infinitely elastic.

Most of Gabe's life had been spent in hospitals, being hooked up to machines, coughing so hard he would shove his intestines into his thigh or rupture something in his lung and spew blood into the bathroom sink; he'd had numerous operations, and required between twenty and thirty different medications, depending on the month. Cystic fibrosis, a mutation of the gene that regulates sweat, mucus and digestive enzymes (called the *cystic fibrosis transmembrane conductance regulator*), affects more than just the lungs—it also impairs the liver and pancreas, leading to diabetes, pancreatitis, and malabsorption; the heart, gall bladder, intestines, and reproductive organs are also affected to varying degrees, depending on the specific mutation (there are over 1,500). It is an incredibly expensive disease: Gabe's medical bills were regularly five and occasionally six figures. His medication alone cost thousands each month, and a "good deal" for the vest he used for breathing treatments was $5,000. Thankfully, because cystic fibrosis is classified as a childhood disease (historically, patients did not live long into adulthood), many of his bills were covered by the Bureau for Children with Medical Handicaps (BCMH), a state-funded program operated by the Ohio Department of Health. Along with Medicaid, however, this program frequently found itself on the chopping block in the name of balancing the budget, so it was never certain he would continue to receive this financial support.

Gabe's only chance at surviving was a double lung transplant (a single lung transplant would not work because the diseased lung would infect the healthy one). One of his lungs had collapsed the previous year, sending him to the hospital for several months—for which he received a bill of nearly a half million dollars. He was alone when it collapsed, but somehow managed to call an ambulance, unlock his patio door, and lie on the floor to wait for the EMT to arrive. When they did, the technician jammed a tube directly into his chest, a blindingly painful moment that ultimately saved his life. He had made a remarkable recovery since his stay in the hospital, but his health was on a steady decline. His weight had dropped to about 95 pounds, despite a 4,000 calorie-a-day diet, and his movements were markedly diminished: once able to walk freely, he could now barely make it to the car without being out of breath. He needed small oxygen tanks when he left the house, and I was often in charge of carrying them from the house to his trunk.

"I'm on the list," he told me one day, meaning that he had finally made it to the transplant list. The only thing left to do, at that point, was wait—wait for someone else to die, someone with lungs that would fit Gabe's small frame (a small woman or a child, most likely), or wait for Gabe himself to die, which increasingly seemed like a strong possibility.

With nothing else to do, we spent our days driving the rural landscapes of Ohio, circling the country roads until we didn't know where we were anymore. I often drove with him to hospital appointments in Columbus and we would take remote back roads as if in search of something we hoped might present itself, there in the middle of nowhere. For Gabe, I think, this something was a sense of purpose amidst the pain and agony and contingency a life with chronic illness had given him. He had spent his childhood convinced he wouldn't live to see twenty, living dangerously because he thought it wouldn't make a difference; now, he just wanted to change things in whatever way he could. He began to write a regular blog online, hoping to connect with other people with cystic fibrosis or any other sort of chronic illness. He rediscovered his religious faith, and to help with the costs of the surgery that would have mostly fallen on his family, he held a fundraiser in the basement of his church.

Eventually, Gabe was too sick to leave his house. He was on oxygen all the time, dragging small tanks with him whenever we went to appointments, which was the only time he left the house. Mostly, I visited him in his room, where he spent his days doing near-constant breathing treatments and playing video games to pass the time (because of the diminished oxygen, he could no longer concentrate enough to read). One day, he entered the hospital at the Cleveland Clinic—where he had gone to be reevaluated for his lung transplant, to make sure he was still healthy enough to have the surgery.

"I'm leaving here with new lungs," he said. "Or I'm not leaving at all."

The first call came a short time later: lungs had arrived, and he was preparing for surgery. After an hour, I received a second call that the surgeon had looked at the lungs and discovered they weren't good. They had either been damaged in transport or were not a proper match. A few weeks passed, and Gabe was being prepped for surgery again. Once more, it didn't happen: the lungs were no good. I visited him and, before I left, embraced him, wondering if it would be the last time I saw him alive: his lungs were filling with fluid that, when coughed into a small container, stunk vaguely of urine. The stench was a visceral signal of death.

A week or so later, Gabe entered surgery and, to the surprise of the doctors involved in the transplant—who upon looking at his damaged internal organs questioned whether he would make it through the procedure—he awoke the following day with a fresh set of lungs tucked inside his chest and a massive scar down the center of his abdominal cavity where they had opened him. He emerged from the hospital, a month later, his skin no longer jaundiced but now sensitive to sunlight. (One side effect of his immunosuppressant was a drastically increased risk of skin cancer, something he embraced because it allowed him to continue wearing his massive hoodies; as he jokingly reminded me, "It makes me look more goth.") His cough was gone, that head-crushing explosion that rattled from deep inside of his chest and made those around him instinctively step away out of fear of contamination.

After he had recovered from his transplant, Gabe and I continued our journeys around Ohio. During one of our drives, he turned to me and said, as if suddenly remembering: "My mother dated your father. I don't know why I never thought of that before."

"You're serious!" I said.

"When they were younger," he laughed. "Isn't that insane?"

"Yeah," I said. It seemed too impossible not to be true.

"We're basically related," he joked. "Like cousins or something."

It began to rain, and Gabe rolled down the window. He stuck his hand out, collected the rain in his palm and wiped it on his face. He collected more and drank it, as though allowing the Ohio countryside to baptize him in his new life. For a brief moment, things seemed to be working out.

It wouldn't last long. I moved away to enroll in a graduate program, in philosophy, in part to continue deferring my loans, and Gabe and I were forced to communicate remotely and catch up during the holidays. Eventually, after marrying a woman he thought was his soul mate, Gabe was diagnosed with skin cancer, most likely caused by the immunosuppressant he took to prevent his body from rejecting his lungs.

A short time later, Gabe's wife left him and he began drinking heavily. His decline was rapid, and reminded me of my father's. He continued to drink, and during a visit home from Chicago, where I had since moved, I stopped by to see him shortly before Christmas. At one point, he disappeared into a side room, emerging a few moments later holding a shotgun. It looked old, like one of those double-barreled pigeon shooters you see in a cartoon. He snapped the barrel shut with a quick thrust of his arm and pointed it at me. "It's an antique," he said. "The same gun Hemingway used to kill himself." I laughed, and after he asked me if I wanted to hold it, we spent the evening discussing love and literature and the upcoming 2016 election. We made plans to attend a concert in April. I drove back to Chicago a few days later, not knowing that I would never see him again. On the ninth anniversary of my father's death, alone in a house he had bought with his wife, Gabe committed suicide at the age of 33.

I have thought a lot about Gabe's life in the years since his death. About how complicated it was, and about how he became a statistic in a tragic epidemic: in Ohio, like most states, suicide rates rose over 30 percent between 2014 and 2016, and along with Gabe, that year almost 45,000 other Americans decided to end their lives.[1] Mostly, I have thought about how Gabe's life was one in which someone ostensibly did "everything right." He "overcame" his chronic illness and, through sheer will and stubborn resolve, put himself through college, through the grueling process of law school. He became a practicing lawyer, married, and bought a house with his wife. He was, in many ways, a shining proof of the American Dream, that wonderful ideal of individual triumph over adversity that has intoxicated the poor with the belief they, too, could become successful. They just need the proper bootstraps. They would also, it goes without saying, do well with something or someone to blame when the machinations of an indifferent economy and ruthless political calculus invariably contradict whatever life they imagine for themselves: immigrants, minorities, feminists, elitist liberals, big government bureaucrats.

But Gabe's story was, to start with, not one of individual triumph. He was, at all times, supported by a network of friends and family. He was also fortunate enough to have financial support from both the federal government and the state of Ohio that prevented him and his family from being completely destitute—although even this support was not enough to prevent the stresses of financial worry, and it certainly did not cover expenses that fell outside the scope of an insurance claim: the many thousands of tanks of gas used to drive him to the hospital, the food consumed without ceremony or pleasure on the road, the cost of housing during the years before the transplant. Had Gabe lived in another state, or had any of those programs he counted on been cut as many beating the drum of "socialized medicine is tyranny" would have preferred, it is likely that he would not have lived as long as he did. His story of triumph could have easily become the all-too-familiar story of falling through the massive cracks in our safety net.

Gabe's story did end in tragedy, but a tragedy of a different kind. Here, the story of individualism and determination becomes something quite different: Gabe's suicide was a choice, one that he alone made, and for this reason, we should feel heartbroken that someone with so much potential had decided his life was not worth living. But, and this is the second thing about Gabe's story that needs considering, we are conditioned to feel this way because Gabe was "worthy": an educated professional, someone with the trappings of a middle-class life. Within our present cultural and political context, his was a life that mattered. But not all lives do. One of the primary effects of the culture wars over the last few decades is the way they have helped to rationalize the suffering and exploitation of "out-groups," which is to say those belonging to some identity or culture deemed expendable because of their so-called "values." Such ideas encourage us not to examine the structures in which human beings operate and make choices about these values, but rather simply to feel something about them: people are good and worthy people, or else they are vile, backward miscreants and criminals who might as well do us all a favor and die off.

Workers, of course, have long been expendable within the framework of class warfare—capitalism requires they remain superfluous to keep wages low, among other reasons. But any understanding of this fact is generally neglected in favor of the much easier critiques of personal beliefs. In an op-ed for the *Washington Post*, for example, titled "Every Story about Trump Supporters I Have Read in the Past Week," Alexandra Petri effectively laughed at precarious labor and unemployment to poke fun at sentimental portrayals of Trump supporters:

> In the shadow of the old flag factory, Craig Slabornik sits whittling away on a rusty nail, his only hobby since the plant shut down. He is an American like millions of Americans, and he has no regrets about pulling the lever for Donald Trump

in November—twice, in fact, which Craig says is just more evidence of the voter fraud plaguing the country. Craig is a contradiction, but he does not know it. Each morning he arrives at the Blue Plate Diner and tries to make sense of it all. The regulars are already there. Lydia Borkle lives in an old shoe in the tiny town of Tempe Work Only, Ariz., where the factory has just rusted away into a pile of gears and dust. The jobs were replaced by robots, not shipped overseas, but try telling Lydia that.

This is an effective jab at the paternalism and pathos that characterizes bad liberal journalism, and clichéd sentimental writing generally. But Petri offers nothing approaching a solution to the problem it takes as its object, instead contenting herself with an affective release that leaves the world as it is—a joyous, cathartic "fuck you." By passing over the structures that produce or make possible the problem—a system of exploitation that reduces individuals to fungible character "types" and that a profit-driven media industry appropriates for sentimental puff pieces—she merely reproduces the problem with the caveat that she, and everyone reading, knows better. More importantly, her satire uses what is supposed to be an attack on sentimental journalism to take cheap shots at the misfortune and backwardness of its subjects. Isn't it just *hilarious* that these people can find "Tempe Work Only," and that they are too stupid to understand the flaws of their own logic? In the end, the problem for Petri is not that our economy has made them expendable. The problem is that people seem to care that they are suffering.

Politics is not personal. It doesn't matter how Petri or the readers of her op-ed feel about the people they find backward or deplorable, and it doesn't matter what those people feel about someone like me, whom they would probably consider an elitist academic commie, or about people who don't look like them.

Changing hearts is a worthy project, but it is not a viable politics. Too often, it neglects the material conditions in which these beliefs are formed, ascribing them instead to individual will and requiring a similarly neoliberal "bootstrapping" into the proper worldview: just change your thoughts and feelings, and if it isn't obvious, then you should try getting educated and recognizing the error of your ways. As though centuries of injustice were ever about making a conscious choice to feel one way or another; as though it matters what the financiers of crisis feel about the people who suffer as a result of their actions to maintain or increase their power.

To those suspicious of such indifference to identity, I will add what should be obvious: racism is a problem. So is sexism, and homophobia, and xenophobia, and any form of oppression perpetuated against a specific community of human beings. But getting everyone to feel a certain way about these problems will not end the sufferings of those groups, a great deal of which is economic in nature (for example, the wage gap between both the white and non-white communities and between men and women, or the brutal exploitation of migrant labor, or the high rates of homelessness experienced by LGBTQ people). The claim that class politics is "economically reductionist" because it privileges labor over identity and culture should be recognized for precisely what it is: red-baiting. Rather than offering a vision for resisting the oppressive logic of capitalism and the elites that profit from it, such ideas direct attention away from the true cause of suffering—a profit-hungry society, its state institutions, and its policies of austerity and violence.

Without a commitment to ending the meritocracy of the market, and the cultural perceptions it encourages us to accept, we invariably begin to decide that some lives are more valuable than others. We acquiesce, and rather than dismantling systems of oppression, we merely redirect that oppression onto others: often, the so-called dregs of society, those whose damaged lives are an indictment of the deep sickness that is liberal capitalism; the people liberals might call white trash and rednecks; the people conservatives might call thugs and addicts and immigrants; the people I have spent much of my life attempting to understand; the people I've called my family and friends.

One day, after having been back in Ohio for some time, I received a call from Kevin, my old roommate from Bowling Green. He was living outside Toledo now, coincidentally in the same apartment complex where my father and Cynara lived shortly before she was diagnosed with cancer in 2004. When I answered, he was crying. He was depressed and suicidal. Although the opioid epidemic would not become "newsworthy" for another five or six years— when other predominately uneducated whites would receive a fashionable amount of pity during the 2016 election cycle, only to be subsequently mocked by people insisting they deserved their fate and quickly forgotten after Trump's win—Kevin was already a tragic representative of this epidemic. He was spending most of his savings on Vicodin, OxyContin, and Percocet, and at the height of his addiction, was snorting or swallowing around thirty pills throughout the day (his liver, he would soon discover, was damaged to the point that his body was simply not breaking down much of what he was putting into it, which was compounded by the fact that he had permanently altered his pain receptors to require opioids). As I did with my father, I felt a responsibility to Kevin, a need to save him.

Still without a car of my own, I borrowed my mother's car on a day she had no appointments and drove up to visit him. When I arrived, he was lying on his sofa, beneath a large blanket. We sat for a bit, watching television. After a while, he sat up and opened an enormous pill bottle and dumped the contents on the coffee table, hundreds of little tablets that may have lasted him a month. I don't think he ever left his apartment anymore, except to score more pills. He raked through the pills in front of him as if it were a meditation garden, laughing a little as he swept them back into piles and returned the piles to the bottle.

He leaned back, taking a deep breath. "It hurts," he said, pointing to his stomach. "Right here. You ever get that?"

"Heartburn," I said.

He shook his head and laughed a little. "Everything hurts. I gotta quit this stuff." He held up a bottle of pills and shook it, like it was a rattle. Then he let out a long, defeated sigh. "You want to watch a movie or something?"

He put on *Vanilla Sky*, a film we had watched countless times as roommates. I smoked a few cigarettes and Kevin curled up under his blanket again. Soon, the film came to the moment Kevin and I often quoted to each other: when David Aames, played by Tom Cruise, is presented with a "facial prosthetic" for his severely disfigured face.

"The aesthetic replacement does work," a doctor tells him. "Emotionally. And actually."

"And," another adds, "the plastic in the aesthetic shield also blocks out abusive rays and assists in the regeneration of cells."

"So it's an aesthetic regenerative shield," Aames responds, toying with them.

"And the ergonomics of the plate barrier allows it to interact reflexively with the movements of your own face," a third doctor adds.

Looking back, this exchange seems appropriate, in many ways, to the world Kevin and I had been born into, one of fierce and uncompromising neoliberalism: the problem Aames had was that he was damaged. He had been in an accident, and he was in pain. He was disfigured. And although he was wealthy and vain and entitled enough to believe he could fix it, the reality is that the meaning of his suffering had been denied. The magic of technology, he thought, would offer a solution. It is hardly a leap from this to the magical thinking at the core of our present worldview. For those of us who are in pain, who are damaged, the causes are as endless as they are obvious: we are working highly exploitative jobs for little money and no benefits, and cannot imagine ourselves ever being freed from the shackles of medical debt and student loans; our political landscape appears rotten with malfeasance, self-interest, and corporate influence; our planet, trapped in a paradigm of infinite growth that requires the brutal exploitation of natural resources, is barreling towards collapse; most of us, quite simply, cannot imagine a future in which there is anything but more suffering, and of worse kinds. The response of those in power is not so different from that of Aames's doctors: vague market-speak meant to assure us things will be fine, technocratic palliatives that deny us the reality of our pain. Pointing to the "innovations" of gig economy grifts and precarious labor, they promise that these are the masks that will heal us—emotionally, and actually.

At the end of the film, Aames realizes that everything after that meeting with the doctors has been a lucid dream, a fantasy he has created for himself, a place where he could exist while his body remained suspended somewhere between life and death. He must choose, in the end, to continue living in his fictitious life or open his eyes to a world now vastly different—to go home again, with the caveat that after 150 years, his wealth would be significantly less valuable.

I looked at Kevin, skeletal and almost emotionless on his sofa. Shortly after my father's death, I remembered, he had shown up at my apartment with $100 worth of groceries. After living together for so many years, he knew exactly what to buy. Then we sat in my apartment, not talking about anything. He was sober and very proud of it. Now, our roles reversed, he reached for the remote and silently turned off the film, rolling slowly into an upright position and lighting a cigarette. He nervously flicked the butt and tapped it against the ashtray. He fidgeted with his sleeves. His hands, I noticed, were bloody and cracked, the skin hardened over and beginning to break.

"I wash my hands probably thirty times a day now," he explained. He looked at the back of his hands as if in disbelief.

Kevin's problem was that he did not know how to stop. Despite treatment facilities and interventions, he couldn't bring himself to let go. He tried killing himself multiple times, but even that didn't work. The first was with a bottle of aspirin; he woke up the next day, maybe because his liver was so destroyed from his addiction to painkillers that it all went right through him, or maybe because, after living with so much pain, he was finally granted something like dumb luck. He tried again later, downing dozens of pills, but immediately changed his mind, quickly jamming a large straw down his throat to make himself retch it up.

He turned to me suddenly. "You fish?"

I shook my head. "Not really a fisher."

He gestured at two fishing poles propped in the corner. "Fish with me," he said. "My grandpa gave me those."

So, we wandered outside, towards the small, man-made pond behind the large apartment complex where residents could fish. After only a few yards, the pole in my hand fell apart. We both looked at in disbelief. I let out a laugh and Kevin shrugged.

"I guess you'll just have to watch me fish," he said.

We sat in the grass, the gray interstate that connects Detroit to Toledo, Findlay, and Cincinnati at our backs. Kevin cast into the pond, and we lit our cigarettes and made small talk. He was going to find another job, somehow. He just had to get his shit together. It sounded like the same things my father said to me shortly before his death: performances meant to assure everyone he was fine, really. He just needed a little time. It sounded like every person I had ever known, struggling to find a way to get out of debt and into a dignified life, talking oneself into it with the hope that it might finally happen.

It would not happen for Kevin. In about a year, his addiction would worsen. He would begin using heroin, first snorting it as he did with pills and later injecting it between his toes. Eventually, he found himself at treatment center in Michigan run by Scientologists who had tricked him into signing up by promising him free treatment (his insurance would not cover more stays in rehabilitation clinics). He left after a week, terrified by their bizarre mindfulness techniques, returned to Ohio, and continued using. During another visit, as he struggled to get sober, he spent an hour teaching me the proper technique for picking up boxes to avoid injury. ("You want to feel a burn in your legs," he told me. "This way you know you're not lifting with your back. I've seen a lot of people hurt themselves that way.") Then, he asked me to help him flush his heroin down the toilet, and we huddled together in the bathroom. He removed a small plastic bag from his pocket and opened it, dumping what was left of his heroin into the water. Sighing, he flushed it, and we watched as the swirling tide carried the stuff away.

On this day, well before that time, Kevin's fishing line got caught on something beneath the surface.

"Hold this," he said, handing me his pole.

He stood and rolled his pants up to his thighs, revealing legs that were the palest of anyone I'd ever seen, the veins all sinewy and raised. Slowly, he put one foot in after the other, sloshing deeper and deeper until the water reached his waist. Kevin gave me a defeated look and held up the torn line. He sloshed out, sopping wet, and sat beside me.

"Too bad," I said.

He lit another cigarette and shrugged. "Can't save everything, I guess."

"No," I told him, "you can't."

"What a crazy place this world is." He laughed in disbelief. "I think about that a lot."

"Yeah," I said. "Me too."

After a long silence, he shrugged and wondered, "What can you do?"

In 2012, Kevin left a suicide note on his brother's kitchen table and stole his television, selling it to buy one last bag of heroin. He found a parking lot somewhere in the decaying city of Toledo and attempted to overdose. He nodded off, drifted away, and awoke to a police officer knocking on his window. Instead of arresting him, the cop, in a moment of mercy, took him home. Kevin underwent more treatment, and in 2013 we sat together in a coffee shop where he told me, with a look I will never forget, that the only two things he could think about were death and heroin.

"I think about death a lot, too," I told him.

And I would continue to think about it, over the years. I thought about it with each impossible attempt to imagine a future for myself. I thought about it in 2016 when Gabe took his life, and I thought about it a few weeks after Donald Trump took office as a champion of the poor and the forgotten, of the so-called "white working class" imagined by the media as a wretched, uneducated mob. On February 7, 2017, Kevin overdosed on heroin and died in his apartment in Columbus. He had been sober for a few years, and his body simply couldn't go on any longer. He was 34 years old. His obituary, like Gabe's, like my father's, can be found online. "Died at his residence," they all say: a carefully constructed phrase that functions to disguise the fact someone died one of those dreaded "deaths of despair," and did so alone.

I did not attend Kevin's funeral. After Gabe's death, I could not bring myself to see another one of my friends on their backs, looking only vaguely the way he did in life. I could not bring myself to grapple with the question of why I "made it" and they did not. There were many chances for me to turn out like my father, like Gabe and Kevin, and the only explanation for why it never happened is an explanation that is rarely satisfying: I was lucky. By chance, not by personal will or determination, did I find myself where I am. In a system that produces widespread precariousness, luck is most often the real difference between success and failure, between life and death. To accept this fact is to accept the utter stupidity of a world we have internalized as natural. It is to accept that, for too many, there is no home for us here, no promise that such a fate will not befall us.

As I write this, there is no guarantee that it will not still happen to me. Perhaps this is the reason I often find myself returning to that warm afternoon with Kevin, replaying our time together, wishing I could go back for even a few minutes to a time that, despite everything, allowed me to believe everything might still be okay.

After sitting by the lake for an hour, Kevin walked me to my car, his pants legs still wet and rolled up above his knees. Still holding his fishing pole in one hand, he waved to me from the sidewalk, an exaggerated, comical performance he often repeated when we went our separate ways.

"Bye, Adam," he shouted. "Bye," he kept waving. "Bye."

I laughed and pulled away. As I left, I passed the building where my father and Cynara lived, the place they left behind before moving to Pennsylvania, before having no place to live, before dying. The last place, I think, they could ever call a home.

Epilogue: The Stories We Tell

At the end of 2017, about ten months after Kevin died, I found myself spending a day in Libby, Montana. For most of the summer, I had been struggling with Kevin's death, with Gabe's death, and with my own profound sense of hopelessness as I attempted to imagine a life among the ruins of late capitalism. My student loan debt had reached $160,000, much of it interest, and after a short but disastrous relationship I had begun drinking heavily and found myself frequently contemplating suicide. A clumsy attempt early in the summer had, fortunately, failed, leaving me persistently numb and feeling as though I had fallen in so deep that nothing seemed to matter (indifference, I might reiterate, is a common response to despair and alienation). I did, however, have a decent credit line after years of my provider increasing it as a reward for being a "valued member" of their interest-accruing class of debtors. So, I charged a flight to Idaho to visit a friend, and we took a road trip through the top of the state.

I had never been to this part of the country, and I was in awe of both its beauty and, at times, its strangeness. Crossing the Idaho–Montana state line on u.s.-2, just past a small store, a single telephone booth stood at the edge of the highway, surrounded by massive wilderness. The sight of this object, preserved from an earlier era, seemed to embody so much of the region: pragmatism, thriftiness and simplicity, isolation. The lack of cell phone reception in the area presumably made land lines a necessity, so keeping a telephone booth near the edge of a highway made sense. It may not have worked, but it emerged from the fog as if to invite me to enter. I felt curiously compelled to call someone. Perhaps this was simply an effect of isolation, of driving through mountains that were as old as time—that operated on geological timescale, not the manufactured time organized by capital. I thought of the wire that connected to the receiver, how it made literal the entire structure of communication, of connecting one person to another far away, how we have so relentlessly sought to conquer time and space. I thought of the disappearance of telephone cords, a metaphor at once heavy-handed and, in that moment, very relevant. It was as if I had traveled to the past, where my younger self was still in Ohio, and where my father was still alive and writing letters that only a few people would ever read.

Many of the places I visited in Idaho and Montana felt this way: untouched by development and suburbanization, preserved communities operating on their own time. Libby was no different. My friend dropped me off a day before my return train arrived (I had always wanted to take a train through Montana), and I spent the afternoon wandering the empty streets alone, a flaneur in a town that was nearly empty. It was a Sunday, which meant most of the establishments were closed. I settled on hanging out at an old tavern downtown, where I imagined I might meet people. Behind and above the bars hung flat-screen televisions, on which a football game had the attention of the half dozen or so patrons. A small side room was filled with slot machines, where an old man was mindlessly feeding money into one and pulling the lever, and at the back, near the empty pool tables, chicken and beef simmered in crockpots next to a package of tortillas and cups of cheese lettuce, tomatoes, and sour cream.

"They're for watching the games today," the bartender told me when I ordered my drink. "Help yourself if you're hungry."

Libby is tucked neatly into the Rocky Mountains at the western edge of Montana. Like much of the region, it has become extremely conservative, and seems to attract a very particular brand of libertarianism: Ruby Ridge, the site of Randy Weaver's 1992 standoff with the FBI, is only a two-hour drive away, as is the cabin where Ted Kaczynski constructed his bombs and wrote the "Unabomber Manifesto," *Industrial Society and its Future*. Lincoln County, of which Libby is the county seat, voted 72–22 for Trump, with an additional 4 percent of the vote going to Gary Johnson. Behind the bar, I noticed on the door of a cooler filled with bottled beer two signs: one said "Military Veterans for Trump," and the other, "Hillary for Prisoner." I would have had to walk around Libby for quite some time before bumping into a vocal Democrat—although Bernie Sanders performed exceptionally well in this part of the country during the primaries, where his crossover appeal to independent voters was evident.[1]

Most people have probably never heard of Libby. Those who have, likely know it for the devastation wrought by nearby vermiculite mines, which became the subject of several books and many articles by investigative journalists. A sparkling material used in construction, vermiculite contains the dangerous mineral asbestos. After the mining corporation W. R. Grace and Company bought the nearby vermiculite mine in the early twentieth century, the town of Libby was built largely with its byproducts. As a result, Libby residents have an extremely high rate of asbestosis, a hardening of the lung walls that creates breathing difficulties, and other diseases related to prolonged asbestos exposure. Out of a total population of roughly 2,600, hundreds have died of asbestosis and more than a thousand have been diagnosed. The rate of lung disease broadly is between forty and sixty times the national average.[2] Despite overwhelming evidence to suggest otherwise, W. R. Grace and Company was acquitted in 2009 of knowingly endangering the community and attempting to cover up its knowledge of the health risks of vermiculite.

"They knew," Greg insisted when I mentioned it. "I've seen the documents."

Greg was a tall, bald man who had spoken to me as we smoked together outside the bar. He worked for a local company hired by the Environmental Protection Agency (EPA) to manage the clean-up process after the agency declared Libby and the nearby town of Troy a public health emergency. Over the last decade, over $425 million in superfund money had gone into cleaning up the asbestos in the area. It was a time-consuming process, and one to which some residents had shown some resistance—particularly those with a considerable amount of land, as the clean-up requires digging up the soil and analyzing it to determine the concentration of asbestos. While the ongoing clean-up was making the town much safer, Greg and many others were likely to lose a reliable source of income: the EPA had been a major employer for the town, but as soon as the clean-up was finished, their jobs would no longer be needed. Despite this, and despite his insistence that it was a private company that led the cover-up of the vermiculite mine's health risks, Greg's attitude was, at its core, a fierce libertarianism, one he no doubt shared with many of the people in the town: less government, less invasion of privacy, more private enterprise. But why would someone like Greg, who had witnessed firsthand what the quest for profit can do to a community, to the beautiful landscape he admired, champion the very laissez-faire logic that made it possible?

In the popular version of this story, this is where I, the enlightened writer, construct a portrait of Greg as a Trump-loving, white working-class libertarian who cannot see that he is being "duped" into supporting these policies. To suggest he is not so different from me (the implicit assumption being that my position is the correct one), I might add that Greg and I both spent our childhoods in Ohio. I'll describe how he wore a thick Carhartt jacket, even inside, and how he reminded me very much of my extended family: plain-spoken, slightly reserved but unafraid to speak his mind if asked. I will certainly include that he identified as a hunter, and that at times was compelled to perform his masculinity—noting how at one point, in the middle of our conversation, he suddenly declared, "I'm straight, by the way," as though concerned his having a beer with a younger man might suggest otherwise. Then, as I have been taught "good writing" is supposed to do, I will complicate this picture by adding that Greg loves philosophy, and that he himself feels out of place in a town of people he perceives as uneducated and disinterested in critical thought. I will not, to be sure, reflect on the ways this very novel difference smuggles in a predictable sort of paternalism, as though I am patting Greg on the back for having the audacity not to be two-dimensional.

The failure of these kinds of stories is that they are precisely the problem they imagine themselves to be solving: rather than dealing with the material conditions that shape and make possible contradictory beliefs, it relegates them to subjective experience and treats them as a problem of mistaken perception. Indeed, since Trump's election, scores of studies and op-eds have attributed his success to the vagaries of "whiteness," with the implicit claim that people are driven to vote against their economic interests because they privilege their identity and the experience it makes possible. Sure, they benefit from government programs and federal aid, but what "really" matters to them is their race. A column at *Politico*, borrowing from the writings of W.E.B. Du Bois and the psychological "wage" offered by whiteness, insists on precisely this. "White identity," the author writes, "pays dividends you can easily bank, and some that you can't," meaning there are benefits that are not reducible to economic gain.[3] The *New York Times* offers several related answers, from partisanship ("party affiliation has become an all-encompassing identity that outweighs the details of specific policies"[4]) to the psychological phenomenon of "last place aversion," which they describe as "the phenomenon in which relatively low-income individuals oppose redistribution because they fear it might differentially help a 'last-place' group to whom they can currently feel superior.'"[5] No one wants to be in "last place," which is to say they are fine with being poor as long as someone else is slightly poorer.

Here, the issue of class lurks: being "last place" only makes sense if it can be measured materially. Even the uncritical *Psychology Today* understands this, pointing towards the resentment the "have-nots" feel towards the "haves."[6] And as the *New York Times* article goes on to note, the "more important issue" is one of deservingness: the article quotes Lars Lefgren, an economist at Brigham Young University:

> Individuals are more willing to vote for redistribution when they perceive the recipients as being deserving. By this I mean that the recipients are willing to work hard but were experiencing bad luck that left them in need of assistance.

Unfortunately, the deeper implications of this research are passed over. As I have argued throughout this book, this meritocratic conception is a symptom of class inequality that is obfuscated by notions of culture and identity: it is not that class war takes the form of culture war, but rather that the culture wars, including the popular movements that fall under the umbrella of identity politics, have inadvertently (or not) become a way to rationalize and naturalize class war. When you live in a society that praises meritocracy and insists that individual talent and hard work are all that prevent you from success, you are going to need some way of squaring this with reality. The *New York Times* comes achingly close to grasping this when they note that the distinction between deserving and non-deserving communities "often translates into a differentiation between poor whites and poor minorities."[7] Rather than a critique of the ways in which race, culture, or identity reinforce class inequality, we have hand-wringing about how people can be so foolish as to vote for politicians who will likely make their lives worse.

But of course, it is very possible some people are not voting against their interest. If they have an interest in, say, ensuring people don't get abortions, then they know quite well why they are voting for the politician they support. If that is what matters to them, not taxing the rich or funding public institutions, then the contradiction disappears—even if we who presume to know better may not understand or agree with their beliefs. To frame this as "voting against one's interest" takes for granted a fundamentally liberal framework in which it is only a contradiction if it produces an outcome we happen to disagree with (we do not, generally, scold rich people who vote "against their interest" for higher taxes, because, after all, this is a principled reason to vote). From such a viewpoint, voters themselves should be criticized for making the "wrong" decisions, rather than the larger political and economic framework in which these decisions are being made. We may not like their stance on abortion, but to frame it as simply "the reason" they vote for austere economic policy—even if that is the case—concedes enormous political ground from the outset. Instead of declaring them a lost cause, we should be convincing them that such austere policies are as unjust as abortion, or whatever issue motivates them. Otherwise, they will find their notions of justice and fairness quite readily from other sources.

Here, Republicans have been enormously successful at tapping into deep resentment towards those in power by stoking cultural animosity and deep anxiety about the future of a dying empire. They frame economic inequality as cultural difference (real America vs coastal elites), encouraging people to believe that the problem is not that they are poor but that some people look down on their way of life. They have co-opted the language of "fairness," which structures the discourse of identity, and wielded it in the name of victimhood. Even billionaires are now being asked to be identified as "people of means," because, after all, why should they be attacked simply for who they are (enormously wealthy)? Meanwhile, the Democratic Party has repeatedly fallen back on a centrist politics that, in the process of divesting itself of potential controversy, has disabled itself from saying anything whatsoever. Their "Better Deal" platform introduced in 2018 is watered-down, 1990s-style Clinton triangulation that makes a mockery of the New Deal. Their new slogan, "Better Skills, Better Jobs, Better Wages" is as uninspiring as the Papa John's advertising it appropriately echoes. Even such progressive slogans as Medicare-for-All and a $15 minimum wage leave the fundamental structure of our exploitative capitalist economy unmentioned. Indeed, a $15 minimum wage ($30,000 annually) does not even return workers to the $20 wage they would currently have if wages had risen with productivity.

Added to this, many progressive agendas are driven to the center with means-testing that erects arbitrary cut-offs that invariably alienate those who need help but are considered ineligible due to some abstract fact about their present situation: they make $2,000 too much, or their health condition does not fall within the coverage that some underwriter wrote at the behest of a managerial class determined to ensure profit. To be sure, these cut-offs primarily affect working-class people, as it is they who straddle the precarious line between comfort and insecurity. There is no faster way to create feelings of injustice, rage, and despair than such alienating bureaucracy—especially, I might add, when it reinforces our deeply flawed understanding of class by deciding those with an arbitrary degree of privilege are required to buckle up, do their duty, and partake in the realization of profit by purchasing in the market place what should be owed to them by right. Is it surprising, then, that these same people might resent those who are "fortunate" enough to receive assistance?

"Economic anxiety," maligned by centrists with a curious, giddy satisfaction at every glaring example of racism, is one of the more misunderstood terms to have saturated political discourse in the last few years. It is easy to see how the poor turn on one another in a competition for table scraps. But what about the wealthy? A common response to economic or material analyses is, "How can bigotry be explained by economic anxiety when the wealthy are also bigots?" First, this kind of questioning misses the point, primarily because it uncritically accepts what it means to "have a lot of money." How, I would respond, does one acquire such money? To become wealthy, one must live in a society in which it is possible to become wealthy, and to become wealthy, requires that other people are not. That is fundamental to what it *means* to be wealthy. Or, as conservatives poorly argue to scare voters away from programs of wealth redistribution, "If everyone is rich, no one is rich!" (This is precisely the point, though not in the way they intend it.)

Second, class inequality affects everyone. Yes, rich people are privileged and generally do not actively "worry" about losing their homes or paying bills, but owning property and making investments forces one to be aware of the market's tendency to destabilize and create panic. This is a different sort of worry, but it offers an answer to why people with great wealth continue to insist on accumulating more, why it's "never enough." To say they are merely "greedy" is, again, to frame the problem as one of individual psychology. In fact, they are trapped in the cycle of reproducing the conditions that make their wealth possible, namely an impoverished labor force that must borrow to survive, and be penalized for surviving with interest. Furthermore, they are not immune to the worldview these conditions have naturalized: one where the poor, non-white communities are violent, deviant, and lazy. The one where if you are poor and alienated, it is probably because you didn't try hard enough.

When I boarded a train and left Montana, I wasn't thinking about all of this. My instinct was to write the expected story about Greg: the one about how complicated he was, about his conflicting ideas and his love of philosophy. About how he and I were different, but not "so" different. After writing variations of that tale and reading many others by well-meaning ethnographers, I have realized this is not the story that needs to be told. The story I want to tell is not an anthropological but a political one. It is always, of course, better to think concretely, not to paper over the contradictory ways people understand themselves and attempt to navigate an alienating and often-hopeless, unforgiving world. The personal is political, but the political should not be personal, and it should not be a stage on which we enact the clichéd narrative arcs of storytelling. People who are suffering do not need pity. They do not need hugs, or another sentimental puff piece about their tragic lives, and they do not need an inspirational, tear-jerking video of them to go viral online in order for millions of people to view and share and feel all the good feelings a morally upstanding person feels when confronted with injustice. They do not need nuanced representation in journalism.

Why then have I told my own story here, and the stories of those close to me? One reason is purely structural: having been born in the mid-1980s, my life covers many of the crucial changes that I believe have direct relevance to our present situation. I have witnessed what these changes did to working people all around me, and telling my story provides a framework for this history. In many ways, we still live in the shadow of Reagan, whose policies were either embraced by the Bushes or not seriously challenged by Clinton and Obama. This is not to say that Reagan is responsible for the recurring crises of global capitalism we have experienced, which are endemic to the system, but the worldview he embraced endures in the ways we think about politics today. It dramatically limits what many imagine is possible, including so-called "progressive" democrats that function as gatekeepers preventing a truly class-based politics. Indeed, coming of age during this period had a dramatic impact on my own ability to find my way to a structural understanding of social relations, and were it not for a number of contingent factors, I may not have discovered it.

The other reason I used my story is that I continue to straddle an imagined divide in this country, with one foot in the rural farmland of Ohio and the other in the ivory tower of academia. I wanted honestly to explore my attempts to navigate this divide, as well as my yearning to leave behind my past and embrace a new identity, one deeply influenced by cultural attitudes uncritical of free-market meritocracy. I felt obligated to include the stories of my mother, my father, my stepmother, and my friends, whose struggles and misfortunes are examples of our damaged life under capitalism.

Nevertheless, I remain conflicted about the political implication of telling these types of stories. After all, Reagan and Obama, both great orators, were skilled at weaving tales that stirred voters and left them in awe of their soaring rhetoric, even while they championed policies that made the lives of the sad characters in their stories worse. They translated despair into votes, just as struggling media outlets have used despair to compete for readers and advertising revenue. As the great James Agee once put it, reflecting on his work for *Fortune* magazine,

> It seems to me curious, not to say obscene and thoroughly terrifying, that it could occur to an association of human beings drawn together through need and chance and for profit into a company, an organ of journalism, to pry intimately into the lives of an undefended and appallingly damaged group of human beings, an ignorant and helpless rural family, for the purpose of parading the nakedness, disadvantage and humiliation of these lives before another group of human beings, in the name of science, of "honest journalism" (whatever that paradox may mean), of humanity, of social fearlessness, for money, and for a reputation for crusading and for unbias which, when skillfully enough qualified, is

exchangeable at any bank for money (and in politics, for
votes, job patronage, abelincolnism, etc.); and that these
people could be capable of meditating this prospect without
the slightest doubt of their qualification to do an "honest"
piece of work, and with a conscience better than clear, and in
the virtual certitude of almost unanimous public approval.[8]

Agee was expressing his conflicted feelings as a journalist
detailing the lives of sharecroppers in the aftermath of the Great
Depression, but we have a variety of our own "sharecroppers"
today. Politics has become saturated with storytelling that
imagines the action called for is merely to listen, and especially
to *feel*. There is nothing inherently political about telling stories,
however, especially if these stories are divorced from the material
and historical conditions from which they emerge. Epiphanies and
sentimentality make for great storytelling, but they don't provide
a foundation for political action. It is true, for example, that
people like the many working-class residents of Libby, Montana,
who voted against their "self-interest" by embracing Trump were
voting against their class interests. That is a story one can tell, and
do so with all the effective (and affective) tools. But no amount of
shaming, moralizing, or sympathizing will change the complicated
ways they have come to interpret their place in a bankrupt
hierarchy. Neither, I should add, is getting everyone to like them.
As Walter Benn Michaels writes, "Blaming the victim (treating
poor people as if they were responsible for their poverty) may
be bad, but it's hard to see how congratulating the victim (I love
what you've done with your shack!) is better."[9]

For decades, our already struggling public institutions have
been whittled down or eliminated in the name of austerity and
"efficiency." What we need is not merely "fairness" of the sort
that grievance politics overwhelmingly demands, or the correct
sentiment concerning injustice. We need a healthcare system that
is not driven by the profit motive but that is structured as a truly

public service. We need an educational system freed from the language of "investment," one that will not destroy lives, ambition, and excitement to satisfy boards of trustees and a bloated administrative payroll. What we need is not just a higher minimum wage, or even a living wage (although this would be nice); we need to be released from the tyranny of wage labor altogether, to operate no longer under the assumption that labor is first and foremost an alienating, undignified, and repetitious ceremony we must suffer through to pay bills. What we need is a radically different society, one that does not keep the vast majority of its citizens from meeting their material needs in the name of "economic growth." We don't need our economy to "grow," a term that has encouraged large-scale destruction of the planet and contributed to rapid climate change, the single greatest threat facing our species. We need an economy that is not controlled and managed by a small class of owners, but democratically by those who make an economy possible: workers.

I do not know what all of this would look like, exactly. I don't have the policy proposals that would win over the skeptics, and I don't have an easy solution to the problem of how to change our class structure, which remains as apparently natural and immutable as ever, and which the representatives of capital protect with astonishing resources. But the first step—a small but important one—should be to get people to see, think, and talk about class, freed from the moralizing framework that has obscured it for so long. In what turned out to be his final book, Chris Harman writes:

> Marx made a distinction between a class which exists in itself, as an objective element in the social structure, shaped by the relations of people to the means of making a livelihood, and a class for itself, with a consciousness of its position and of its interests in opposition to those of another class.[10]

We the poor, the workers, the exploited, already exist as a class in itself, even if we remain unable to recognize it as something to which we all belong. The rich and the powerful, meanwhile, exist as a class both in and for itself, their interests clearly defined and broadly shared––whatever competition they may have with each other is bracketed in their collective need to maintain the present structure of society. We, too, must make our interests clearly defined and broadly shared. We, too, must become a class for itself and bracket our difference, not to maintain the structure of society, but to begin to challenge it.

References

Prologue: You Can't Go Home Again

1 Thomas Wolfe, *You Can't Go Home Again* (New York, 1998), p. 698.
2 According to the Social Security Administration's Average Wage Index. Admittedly, this data looks at individual incomes, and doesn't reflect total household income or those with temporary or part-time jobs. But it also doesn't look at those who hold multiple jobs, or whose income, even if above poverty level, is insufficient with respect to cost of living, for example those who live in expensive metropolitan areas like New York City, San Francisco, and Washington, DC, www.ssa.gov, accessed October 2, 2018.
3 According to a Gallup poll conducted on Trump's 500th day in office, his overall approval rating stood at 42 percent, a slight fall from the 45 percent he had after taking office. His support among Republicans, however, was 87 percent, second only to George W. Bush's popularity in the aftermath of the 9/11 terrorist attacks.
4 Even the relatively conservative *Washington Post* reported on this. Nicholas Carnes and Noam Lupu, "It's Time to Bust the Myth: Most Trump Voters were not Working Class," *Washington Post*, June 5, 2017, www.washingtonpost.com.
5 Jesse A. Myerson, "Trumpism: It's Coming From The Suburbs," *The Nation* (May 8, 2017).
6 Barbara Ehrenreich, *Fear of Falling: The Inner Life of the Middle Class* (New York, 1990), p. 110.
7 Robert P. Jones, Daniel Cox, and Rachel Lienesch, "Beyond Economics: Fears of Cultural Displacement Pushed the White Working Class to Trump | PRRI/The Atlantic Report." PRRI (2017).
8 Emma Green, "It Was Cultural Anxiety that Drove White, Working-class Voters to Trump," *The Atlantic* (May 9, 2017) www.theatlantic.com (italics mine).
9 Jones, Cox, and Lienesch, "Beyond Economics."
10 This is one of the major flaws of Joan C. Williams's *White Working Class: Overcoming Class Cluelessness in America* (Boston, MA, 2017).

While overall a thoughtful study on the contradictions that structure white poverty, the book defines the "working class" exclusively by income. In the process, it neglects class relations entirely by truncating all labor below and above an arbitrary limit.

11 Marx offers a similar concept of class in a footnote to the title of the first chapter of *The Communist Manifesto*: "By bourgeoisie is meant the class of modern capitalists, owners of the means of social production and employers of wage labour. By proletariat, the class of modern wage labourers who, having no means of production of their own, are reduced to selling their labour power in order to live." Implicit in these definitions is a relationship that reproduces itself through a mutual but unfair exchange: the workers receive a wage, while capitalists receive profits produced by those workers' labor. At the very end of the third volume of *Capital*, Marx expands on this when he asks, quite directly, "What makes a class?" He first proposes "the identity of revenues and revenue sources," given what he calls the three great social classes—wage-laborers, capitalists, and landowners—receive as the source of their income. But Marx quickly complicates this formula, showing that such a definition of class is still too abstract: "From this point of view, however, doctors and government officials would also form two classes, as they belong to two distinct social groups, the revenue of each group's members flowing from its own source. The same would hold true for the infinite fragmentation of interests and positions into which the division of social labor splits not only workers but also capitalists and landowners—the latter, for instance, into vineyard-owners, fieldowners, forest-owners, mine-owners, fishery-owners, etc." At this point, the manuscript ends, so where Marx would have taken the answer to the question of what makes a class is, unfortunately, impossible to say with certainty. What is clear, however, is that Marx was suspicious of expanding the definition of class to different "fields" of work, as well as limiting it merely to income. See Karl Marx, *Capital: A Critique of Political Economy*, vol. III, trans. David Fernbach (New York, 1981), p. 1026; Karl Marx, Friedrich Engels, and Robert C. Tucker, *The Marx–Engels Reader* (New York, 1972), p. 473.

1 The Era of Big Government Is Over

1 "In this present crisis, government is not the solution to our problem; government is the problem. From time to time we've been tempted to believe that society has become too complex to be managed by self-rule, that government by an elite group is superior to government for, by, and of the people. Well, if no one among us is capable of governing himself, then who among us has

the capacity to govern someone else? All of us together, in and out of government, must bear the burden. The solutions we seek must be equitable, with no one group singled out to pay a higher price." (First Inauguration Speech, Washington, DC, January 20, 1981.)

2 The highest tax rate had been 92 percent from 1951–63, after which it remained between 70 and 77 percent under Johnson, Nixon, Ford, and Carter.

3 My parents had originally wanted to name me Theron Lee Rensch, in honor of these two men, but worried it was too strange of a name and went with Adam instead.

4 Randall Rensch, "An Elite Class Makes America's Decisions," *The Courier* (1992, exact date unknown).

5 The plant closed in 2014, despite receiving a Job Creation Tax Credit and nearly $2 million in clean energy tax credits from the federal government in the 2010s. Meredith Morris, the company's spokeswoman, told the *Toledo Blade* that the decision to close the plant "supports Dow's continued focus on optimizing its resources to create maximum value for the company, its customers, and its shareholders." (Tyrel Linkhorn, "Chemical Company to Close Plant in Findlay," *Toledo Blade* (September 10, 2014).

6 Francis Fukuyama, who advised the Reagan administration (including then Vice President Bush) and assisted in its defense strategy against the Soviet Union, is credited with coining this moment "the end of history." Although his prognosis that history was gradually progressing towards a universal acceptance of liberal democracy and capitalist markets would prove to be incorrect, it is a useful reminder for just how natural and inevitable capitalism appeared after the specter of communism suffered its biggest defeat. As Fukuyama wrote in his 1992 book *The End of History and the Last Man* (New York, 1992): "The apparent number of choices that countries face in determining how they will organize themselves politically and economically has been diminishing over time. Of the different types of regimes that have emerged in the course of human history, from monarchies and aristocracies, to religious theocracies, to the fascist and communist dictatorships of this century, the only form of government that has survived intact to the end of the twentieth century has been liberal democracy."

7 Cf. Sean Wilentz, *The Age of Reagan: A History, 1974–2008* (New York, 2008), p. 310.

8 Sundor made its announcement to close the Findlay plant, along with plants in Chicopee, MA, and Mount Dora, FL, on June 17, 1993. Roughly 350 workers lost their jobs. See Frank Standfield, "Sundor Juice Plant is Closing Next Year," *Orlando Sentinel* (June 18, 1993).

9 Frances Fox Piven and Richard A. Cloward, *Regulating the Poor: The Functions of Public Welfare* (New York, 1993), pp. 353–4.

10 Unlike Iceland and Sweden, which presently have remarkable 91.8 and 67 percent rates, respectively, union membership in the United States peaked at 37 percent in the 1950s. Nevertheless, unions were enormously popular, with almost four out of five Americans having a favorable opinion of union organizing in the workplace. Beginning in the 1960s, however, union membership began its steady decline, and by the 1990s, it had fallen below 15 percent (it is currently at or below 10 percent). The reasons for this are less complex than one might think, and can largely be explained by corporate influence on politicians to weaken labor laws: it is hardly surprising that when wealthy capitalists lobby congress to pass laws in their favor, such laws have a decent chance of being passed. In the 1940s, the passage of the Labor-Management Relations Act, also called the Taft–Hartley Act, weakened bargaining methods by limiting collective action such as strikes, picketing, and boycotts, and allowed states to pass "right-to-work" laws. While the phrase "right-to-work" sounds positive, it, in fact, does not guarantee anyone employment—it merely allows workers to opt-out of paying union dues.

11 Randall Rensch, "What Oxley Didn't Say Is More Important," *The Courier* (1992).

12 Clinton lost the overall white vote to Bush by 2 points (with 21 points going to third-party candidate Ross Perot). However, he won working-class voters overall, despite his tepid support of unions and economic progressivism that emphasized a pro-corporate "invest and grow" language.

13 B. Drummond Ayres, "The 1992 Campaign: Candidate's Record; Unions Are Split on Backing Clinton," *New York Times* (March 15, 1992)

2 White Trash Nation

1 James T. Patterson, *Restless Giant: The United States from Nixon to Bush v. Gore* (Oxford, 2005), p. 169.

2 Heather Boushey, "In Over Our Heads: Debt Burdens, Bankruptcies on the Rise," *Economic Policy Institute* (September 18, 2002), www.epi.org.

3 Paul Mattick, *Business as Usual: The Economic Crisis and the Failure of Capitalism* (London, 2011), p. 59.

4 Peter Edelman, "The Worst Thing Bill Clinton Has Done," *The Atlantic* (March 1, 1997). Robert Reich, Clinton's close friend and Labor Secretary, also criticized the bill for having "no health care or child care for people coming off welfare, no job training, no assurance of a job paying a living wage, nor, for that matter, of a job at any wage," while Christopher Hitchens—before his reactionary

turn—was more direct in his assessment, calling the bill "more hasty, callous, short-term, and ill-considered than anything the Republicans could have hoped to carry on their own," one that "made sure he had robbed them of an electoral issue, and gained new access to the very donors who customarily sent money to the other party." See Christopher Hitchens, *No One Left to Lie to: The Triangulations of William Jefferson Clinton* (London, 2008), p. 28.

5　Here, I am indebted to Marilynne Robinson, who writes in *The Death of Adam* (New York, 2005), p. 83: "I am afraid we also are forgetting that emotions signify, that they are much fuller of meaning than language, that they interpret the world to us and us to other people. Perhaps the reality we have made fills certain of us, and of our children, with rage and grief—the tedium and meagerness of it, the meanness of it, the stain of fearfulness it leaves everywhere. It may be necessary to offer ourselves palliatives, but it is drastically wrong to offer or to accept a palliative as if it were a cure."

6　Nancy Isenberg, *White Trash: The 400-year Untold History of Class in America* (New York, 2016), p. 236.

7　Keith Olbermann tweeted, "Look! Ted Nugent! Sarah Palin! Kid Rock! Future Ex-President Don! It's the next cast of 'Dancing With Trailer Park Trash!'," on April 20, 2017 at 6:32 a.m.

8　Thomas Frank, *Listen, Liberal: or, What Ever Happened to the Party of the People?* (New York, 2016), p. 32.

9　One of the more insidious suggestions by some liberals is that to run for higher office, or to hold any political position, one must pass an IQ test, or show sufficient knowledge of geography and history (in recent years, a joke endlessly made at the expense of Donald Trump's obviously limited knowledge). While this might seem reasonable on the surface, it plays into a troubling conception of aptitude that treats intelligence as genetic, or at the very least a privilege afforded to those fortunate enough to attend elite schools.

10　In fact, as Mariana Mazzucato notes in her book *The Value of Everything* (New York, 2018), pp. 104–11, until about 1970, the financial sector was not even included in GDP calculations because it was not understood to "create" value. Similarly, the cost FISIM (financial intermediation services, indirectly measured) was not included until 1993, when it also was considered to "add" value to the economy (for example, through banks lending money at higher interest rates than that from which they borrow).

11　Columnist David Brooks, himself a centrist, extolled the virtues of this new rising class: "The values of the bourgeois mainstream culture and the values of the 1960s counterculture have merged. That culture war ended, at least within the educated class. In its place that class has created a third culture, which is a reconciliation between the previous two." See *Bobos in Paradise: The New Upper Class and How They Got There* (New York, 2000), p. 43.

3 There Is No Such Thing as Society

1 Clinton's lowest rating (37 percent) occurred in 1993, as he attempted and failed to pass a universal healthcare bill. By the end of 1998, two years after he had passed the welfare reform bill and at the cusp of the "dot.com" bubble, his approval ratings were at 73 percent.

2 As noted by the Economic Policy Institute, "The 1947 Taft–Hartley amendments to the National Labor Relations Act (1935) sanctioned a state's right to pass laws that prohibit unions from requiring a worker to pay dues, even when the worker is covered by a union-negotiated collective bargaining agreement." By their count, this translates to a significant decrease (16–17 percent) in average hourly wages across the board. See Elise Gould and Will Kimball, "'Right-to-work' States Still Have Lower Wages," Economic Policy Institute Briefing Paper #395 (April 22, 2015). Interestingly, New Mexico is not a right-to-work state, despite being surrounded on all sides by states with right-to-work laws (Arizona, Nevada, Utah, Texas, and Oklahoma). Nevertheless, New Mexico's wages are significantly lower, and in some industries (construction, service, education), workers make 20–25 percent less than the u.s. average.

3 Buchanan wanted to "make America first again"; Patrick Buchanan, August 17, 1992, Republican National Convention Speech, accessed at www.c-span.org.

4 Interview with Douglas Keay for *Woman's Own* magazine, October 31, 1987, www.margaretthatcher.org.

5 Walter Benn Michaels, *The Trouble with Diversity: How We Learned to Love Identity and Ignore Inequality* (New York, 2006), p. 199.

6 It became a subsidiary called Marathon Petroleum in 1990, but still maintained a major financial presence, employing over 2,000 people as part of its national, multi-billion-dollar operation (as of 2017, it was still controlling 1.9 million barrels of oil per day).

7 Barbara Ehrenreich, *Nickel and Dimed: On (Not) Getting By in America* (New York, 2001), p. 208.

4 The Culture Wars

1 2A was a short period between 2nd and 3rd that was generally called "home room."

2 Naomi Klein, *Fences and Windows* (New York, 2002), p. 165.

3 Toni Morrison's claim about Clinton being the first black president, published in the *New Yorker* in 1998, is often understood to mean

that Clinton somehow embodied "blackness." In fact, her remark was less a compliment towards Clinton's ability to connect with black voters and more a rebuke of how he'd been treated as a president, specifically regarding the sex scandal involving Monica Lewinsky. "I said he was being treated like a black on the street," she would later say, "already guilty, already a perp. I have no idea what his real instincts are, in terms of race." Nevertheless, the harmful effects of his policies remain the same.

4 Race as a biological category was effectively debunked from many angles after the Second World War, but, nevertheless, remained a folk concept used by politicians. Not surprisingly, advancements in science have brought with them attempts to rescue race from its social construction, most recently in the field of genetics. Those already inclined to believe in a genetic basis for racial difference have been effective at offering bad faith arguments, particularly in online forums, and using such science to justify their bigotry.

5 For a more sympathetic take on the efficacy of identity politics, see Asad Haider's *Mistaken Identity* (London, 2018).

6 For a clear, concise critique of identity politics, see Walter Benn Michaels's *The Trouble with Diversity: How We Learned to Love Identity and Ignore Inequality* (New York, 2006). On the relationship between race and culture, and the distinction between difference and diversity within the legal discourse, see Richard T. Ford's *Racial Culture: A Critique*. Adolph Reed, Jr. has likewise published extensively on race, class, and identity, and his writings provide an indispensable, recent history of how these issues have influenced left politics.

7 Chris Harman, *Zombie Capitalism: Global Crisis and the Relevance of Marx* (London, 2009), p. 273.

8 Christopher Hitchens, "Be It Resolved: Freedom of Speech Includes the Freedom to Hate," November 15, 2006, retrieved from www.youtube.com.

9 Ibid.

10 Ironically, the alt-right's new slogan, coined by Ben Shapiro, has taken up this same arrogant stance: "Facts don't care about your feelings."

11 Interestingly, it has actually fallen for the Republican members of congress. See Ben Myers and Peter Olsen-Phillips, "In Congress, Even Lawmakers' Degrees Are a Partisan Issue: How Higher Education Is Shaping the House of Representatives," *Chronicle of Higher Education* (May 5, 2017), www.chronicle.com.

12 U.S. Department of Education, National Center for Education Statistics (2016). Digest of Education Statistics, 2015 (NCES 2016–14), Chapter Three.

13 Hillary Wething, Natalie Sabadish and Heidi Shierholz, "The Class of 2012: The Labor Marker for Young Graduates Looks Grim," Economic Policy Institute Briefing Paper #340 (May 3, 2012).
14 Ibid.

5 Inheritance

1 Miya Tokumitsu, "In the Name of Love," *Jacobin*, January 12, 2014.
2 Today, the total amount of student loan debt held by American citizens is over $1.6 trillion. Thousands have defaulted on their loans, unable to make the high payments inflated by accrued interest. Forgiveness programs introduced by Barack Obama—hardly radical to begin with—are under assault by the Trump administration, and those saddled with debt they are unable to pay back are faced with the loss of credit, wage garnishing, and the near-constant stress of creditors who have purchased their loans at auction from the government and are given years essentially to harass students for money.

6 Conditions Are Fundamentally Sound

1 U.S. Securities and Exchange Commission and the Commodity Futures Trading Commission, "Findings Regarding the Market Events of May 6, 2010," September 30, 2010, www.sec.gov.
2 "CSI: Credit Crunch," *The Economist* (October 20, 2007), www.economist.com.
3 Overall, outstanding household debt had grown from $818 billion in 1976 to nearly $14 trillion at the end of 2007, primarily the result of mortgages and credit cards. See The Federal Reserve, "Flow of Funds Accounts of the United States: Flows and Outstandings Fourth Quarter 2007," March 6, 2008, www.federalreserve.gov.
4 Associated Press, "Rural America, Overlooked Epicenter of Subprime Mortgage Crisis, Gets Attention from Regulators," *The Oregonian* (October 21, 2014), www.oregonlive.com.
5 Christine Haughner, "Concern for 2009 as Manhattan Real Estate Market Slows," *The New York Times* (October 2, 2008), www.nytimes.com.
6 According to the U.S. Department of Housing and Urban Development's 2017 Annual Homeless Assessment Report (AHAR) to Congress, the homeless population as of 2017 was 553,742, far less than 1 percent of the total population. This is not terrible for an advanced, post-industrial nation of 325 million people, though if you factor in those individuals who are not technically homeless but live in precarious or unstable housing situations, the numbers are much higher. The report itself only defines a homeless person

as "a person who lacks a fixed, regular, and adequate nighttime residence." Millions of Americans do not meet this criteria but are, nevertheless, living in insecure situations: month-to-month leases, staying with friends or relatives, or even owning a home at risk of foreclosure due to declining value and high interest payments.

7 Housing Assistance Council, "Housing an Aging Rural America: Rural Seniors and Their Homes" (October 2014), www.ruralhome. org.

8 Gillian B. White, "Rural America's Silent Housing Crisis," *Atlantic* (January 28, 2015).

7 Deaths of Despair

1 Amy Ellis Nutt, "Suicide Rates Rise Sharply Across the United States, New Report Shows," *Washington Post* (June 7, 2018), www.washingtonpost.com.

Epilogue: The Stories We Tell

1 Sanders performed exceptionally well in Washington, Idaho, and Utah. He also won every county except one in Oregon and most counties in Montana, although the margins there were much slimmer by comparison.

2 Joanna Walters, "Welcome to Libby, Montana, the Town that Was Poisoned," *The Guardian* (March 7, 2009).

3 Joshua Zeitz, "Does the White Working Class Really Vote Against its Own Interests?" *Politico* (December 31, 2017), www.politico.com/ magazine.

4 Amanda Taub, "Why Americans Vote 'Against Their Interests': Partisanship," *New York Times* (April 12, 2017), www.nytimes.com.

5 Thomas Edsall, "Why Don't We Always Vote in Our Self-interest?" (July 19, 2018), www.nytimes.com.

6 Ronald E. Riggio, "Why Do People Vote Against their Best Interests?" *Psychology Today* (December 12, 2017), www.psychologytoday.com.

7 Edsall, "Why Don't We Always Vote."

8 James Agee, *Let Us Now Praise Famous Men* (Boston, MA, 1941), p. 7.

9 Walter Benn Michaels, *The Trouble with Diversity: How We Learned to Love Identity and Ignore Inequality* (New York, 2006), p. 107.

10 Chris Harman, *Zombie Capitalism: Global Crisis and the Relevance of Marx* (London, 2009), p. 332.

Acknowledgments

This book would not have been possible without Paul Mattick, who has been an incredible mentor and editor, and Vivian Constantinopoulos, who allowed me to write the better version of this story. I would also not have become the writer and thinker I am without the many conversations, arguments, and lectures with my friends and colleagues at University of Illinois at Chicago. Walter Benn Michaels, especially, has taught me more than perhaps anyone, and his influence is considerable throughout this book. Many other friends have offered feedback, but two deserve mention here: Daniel Burnfin, whose understanding of political economy is unmatched by anyone I know, and Andy El-Zayaty, who challenges me to always think in a more nuanced manner. Finally, I must thank my mother and sister, whose lives are immeasurably more complicated and deserving of books of their own. And to Tyne, who saved my life: thank you.